MARIANNE MOORE

A COLLECTION OF CRITICAL ESSAYS

Edited by

Charles Tomlinson

Prentice-Hall, Inc. *Englewood Cliffs, N. J.*

A SPECTRUM BOOK

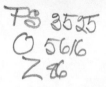

Quotations from the poetry of Marianne Moore used by permission of Dial Press, Inc., Faber & Faber, Ltd., and The Macmillan Company.

Current printing (last number):

10   9   8   7   6   5   4   3   2   1

PRENTICE-HALL INTERNATIONAL, INC. (*London*)
PRENTICE-HALL OF AUSTRALIA, PTY. LTD. (*Sydney*)
PRENTICE-HALL OF CANADA, LTD. (*Toronto*)
PRENTICE-HALL OF INDIA PRIVATE LIMITED (*New Delhi*)
PRENTICE-HALL OF JAPAN, INC. (*Tokyo*)

76433

To Alfred and Beatrice Siegel

Contents

IV. The La Fontaine Translations

V. The Longer View

Introduction: Marianne Moore
Her Poetry and Her Critics

by Charles Tomlinson

I

In an age when such major poets such as Eliot and Yeats have treated nature with an imperiousness that, at times, recalls their symbolist forebears, Miss Moore is ready to accord to objects and to animals a life of their own. "She is lavish and meticulous," Robert Lowell has said. "Her excellence is woman's I think in its worldly concreteness. . . ." [1] This quality, which makes her so different from Eliot and Yeats and draws her closer to the universe of Pound and Williams, depends on an outward-looking interest in fact and detail. Thus, when she came to review Williams' *Collected Poems, 1921–31*,[2] she chose among her instances for approval to quote the specific resistance of:

> a green truck
> dragging a concrete mixer
> passes
> in the street—
> the clatter and true sound
> of verse—

and, further on in the same essay, we are given the following piece of meticulous observation from Williams:

> And there's the river with thin ice upon it
> fanning out half over the black
> water, the free middlewater racing under its
> ripples that move crosswise on the stream.

[1] *Festschrift for Marianne Moore's Seventy-Seventh Birthday,* ed. Tambimuttu (New York: Tambimuttu and Mass, 1964), p. 119.
[2] Miss Moore's review is reprinted in *Predilections* (New York: Viking Press, Inc., 1955), pp. 136–39.

1

The first quotation would appeal readily to a poet who, like Miss Moore, elects to celebrate and to qualify (here she begins to differ from Williams) the irreducible, mechanical presence in "To a Steam Roller." With her, the presence becomes a moral presence, or one that begets nuances of thought where a moral atmosphere asks for definition:

> The illustration
> is nothing to you without the application.
> > You lack half wit. You crush all the particles down
> > > into close conformity, and then walk back and forth
> > > on them.
>
> Sparkling chips of rock
> are crushed down to the level of the parent block.
> > Were not 'impersonal judgment in aesthetic
> > matters, a metaphysical impossibility', you
>
> might fairly achieve
> it. . . .

This ethical extension of fact itself is all her own, and it is something that, as we shall see in the animal poems, distinguishes her approach as fabulist from that of La Fontaine. And for La Fontaine, unlike Miss Moore, the sheer quiddity of animal existence is but a minor concern.

The second quotation from Williams, with its careful attention to the appearance of the iced river, finds its parallel in Miss Moore's capacity to see in an artichoke "six varieties of blue," and also in the way "A Grave" has room, in its sombre trajectory, for those firs "each with an emerald turkey-foot at the top." Similarly, the same trees in "An Octopus" gain definition by the borrowing of Ruskin's phrase, "each like the shadow of the one beside it." Discriminations are present in Miss Moore for "making out," as James would say, the way the thing looked. They are also present for sheer exuberance or humor and simultaneously for an imaginative deepening of the poem's moral implications. In "Four Quartz Crystal Clocks" this alliance of humor and penetration occurs with great charm. The poem appears to deviate at a tangent with the entry of the lemur student, but this turns out, after all, to be precisely to the point:

> > > > Repetition, with
> > > the scientist, should be
> > synonymous with accuracy.
> > > The lemur-student can see
> > > > that an aye-aye is not
> > > an angwan-tibo, potto, or loris. . . .

The unity here of humor and insight, fusing in that notion of accuracy which is being presented, is possible to the kind of poet for whom there is no war between science and poetry, and for whom fact has its proper plentitude. It is this plentitude that supplies the meaningful basis both of poetry and of Miss Moore's earliest interest, biology. She hints at her sense of this unity in her interview with Mr. Hall, reprinted below (pp. 20–51), where she says: "Precision, economy of statement, logic employed to ends that are disinterested, drawing and identifying, liberate—at least have some bearing on—the imagination, it seems to me." It is no surprise to learn from this same interview that she had once thought of taking up medicine, that, in short, she should have found compatibility with two of the least abstract of the sciences. Biology clearly provides a common ground on which eye and mind could come together in harmony. Like Dr. Williams' own medical studies and practice, "drawing and identifying" for Miss Moore in some measure served perhaps to structure and to release the poetic impulse. "Structure" is as important to her as "release," for there is a science of art, and in Miss Moore's own art it is related to care in observing as well as to her scrupulousness over sources and quotations. Samuel Johnson himself, in unexpectedly Moore-like fashion, with his enthusiasm for on-the-spot observations and the noting down of them, saw the affinity of scientific with moral concern, when he wrote, in *A Journey to the Western Islands of Scotland:*

> He who has not made the experiment, or who is not accustomed to require rigorous accuracy from himself, will scarcely believe how much a few hours take from certainty of knowledge, and distinctness of imagery; how the succession of objects will be broken, how separate parts will be confused, and how many particular features and discriminations will be compressed and conglobated into one gross and general idea.[3]

"Particular features and discriminations" stand at the heart of any Moore poem. Yet what of the imaginative flight that goes from the particular to the achieved work of art? How do fact and imagination, at its broadest stretch, learn, in Williams' phrase, to "lie / down together in the same bed," for, though related, they are obviously not synonymous. The poems of wild life are instructive here. They insist often on a primary descriptive accuracy as the ground base for ultimate vision, as in "The Jerboa":

> By fifths and sevenths,
> in leaps of two lengths,
>   like the uneven notes
>   of the Bedouin flute, it stops its gleaning

[3] Samuel Johnson, *A Journey to the Western Islands of Scotland* (Dublin 1775), pp. 239–40.

> on little wheel casters, and makes fern-seed
> foot-prints with kangaroo speed.
>
> Its leaps should be set
> to the flageolet;
>   pillar body erect
>   on a three-cornered smooth-working Chippendale
>   claw—propped on hind legs, and tail as third toe,
>   between leaps to its burrow.

Or, as in "The Paper Nautilus," we are provided with the details of
the way the nautilus "constructs her thin glass shell" to rear her
progeny:

> Giving her perishable
> souvenir of hope, a dull
>   white outside and smooth-
>   edged inner surface
> glossy as the sea, the watchful
>   maker of it guards it
>   day and night; she scarcely
>
>   eats until the eggs are hatched.
> Buried eight-fold in her eight
>   arms, for she is in
>   a sense a devil-
> fish, her glass ramshorn-cradled freight
>   is hid but not crushed.

And the description of the process concludes with the beauty of a
world of fact ramifying out into that of imaginative possibility:

> the intensively
> watched eggs coming from
> the shell free it when they are freed,—
>   leaving its wasp-nest flaws
>   of white on white, and close-
>
>   laid Ionic chiton-folds
> like the lines in the mane of
> a Parthenon horse. . . .

In both "The Jerboa" and "The Paper Nautilus" an ideal of
ethical preference inserts itself among the facts, just as it did in a
different way in Miss Moore's presentation of the steam roller, and in
this insertion the imaginative power kindles to cast light on both the
fact and the ideal. In "The Jerboa," its habitat, the desert, is preferred
to the opulence of the pharaohs because of the ascetic ideal of the
animal's freedom, a freedom which Miss Moore characterises as

"abundance" against the "too much" of ancient Egypt. In "The Paper Nautilus" the mode of protection accords with the ethical extension that "love / is the only fortress / strong enough to trust to." Elsewhere, as in "The Frigate Pelican," man receives his ethical placing simply by the poet's registering that, as Lawrence puts it, "he is not the measure of creation." Lawrence, too, was writing about the animal world, and in "Fish," from which the quotation comes, man is measured by being confronted with "the water-horny mouth . . . the water-precious, mirror-flat bright eye" of the fish. In Miss Moore's "The Frigate Pelican" "we" (that is, we human sight-seers) are placed as we "watch the moon rise / on the Susquehanna," but "this most romantic bird," the pelican, "flies / to a more mundane place, the mangrove / swamp to sleep." We do wrong to humanize everything, to accept only on our own terms the jungle night-fall, "which is for man," she writes, "the basilisk whose look will kill; but is / for lizards man can / kill, the welcome dark." Man, the "less limber animal," with his practical mottoes, must accommodate himself to sea, jungle, frigate pelican, and lizard, and the ethical and the imaginative are one in Miss Moore's animal poems in urging this accommodation.

Different in mode from "The Jerboa" and "The Paper Nautilus" and also from "The Frigate Pelican" is a poem like "Bird-Witted" where the imaginative sharpening comes from an accurately close fit between incident and words. The poem stays close to the incident, the words miming its movements:

> With innocent wide penguin eyes, three
>   large fledgling mocking-birds below
> the pussy-willow tree,
>   stand in a row,
> wings touching, feebly solemn,
> till they see
>   their no longer larger
>   mother bringing
> something which will partially
> feed one of them.
>
> Toward the high-keyed intermittent squeak
>   of broken carriage-springs, made by
> the three similar, meek-
>   coated bird's eye
> freckled forms she comes; and when
> from the beak
>   of one, the still living
>   beetle has dropped
> out, she picks it up and puts
> it in again.

Mr. Kenner comments in detail on this same poem, in his "Meditation and Enactment" below (see pp. 159–64), and, if he is correct, besides heeding the Emersonian prescription, "Ask the fact for the form," Miss Moore is perhaps also engaged in taking up a challenge of Ezra Pound—to equal the bird sounds of Arnaut Daniel. The imaginative effect here is one of mimesis rather than transfiguration or the kind of ethical extension we have encountered elsewhere. The polar opposite of "Bird-Witted" occurs in "Melancthon," the poem about an elephant, though "about an elephant" scarcely says much of the poem's real subject. The title "Melancthon" (Melancthon was a Protestant theologian of the Lutheran Reformation) already alerts us with its obliquity to the controlled fantasy which sets it apart from the poems we have so far discussed. Here the more-than-animal speaks, which is an unusual occurrence in Miss Moore's poetry. Its protestant virtues come, by the middle of the poem, to symbolise the fully human as against "the / wandlike body of which one hears so much," with its fragile prettiness and glassy egotism.

"Melancthon" takes us to the heart of Miss Moore's imaginative exploration of her moral world, a world where spontaneity and order are not at odds and where the marriage between them results in "spiritual poise" rather than the "external poise" of "the wandlike body." An objective symbol of the values proposed in "Melancthon" is to be found in the description the poet gives us of the little town in "The Steeple-Jack." It is the symbol of a social and also a natural mean. The town makes no attempt to impress; it possesses "spiritual poise":

> . . . The church portico has four fluted
> columns, each a single piece of stone, made
> modester by white-wash. This would be a fit haven for
> waifs, children, animals, prisoners. . . .
>
> It could scarcely be dangerous to be living
> in a town like this, of simple people
> who have a steeple-jack placing danger-signs by the church
> when he is gilding the solid-
> pointed star, which on a steeple stands for hope.

Nature is present in "the sweet sea air," the "water etched / with waves as formal as the scales on a fish," in the sea-gulls, the lobsters, the storm that "bends the salt / marsh grass, disturbs stars in the sky and the / star on the steeple," in "the trumpet vine,"

> fox-glove, giant snap-dragon, a salpiglossis that has
> spots and stripes; morning-glories; gourds,
> or moon-vines trained fishing-twine

> at the back
>
> door. . . .

But, to use the subtitles of "The Jerboa," it is natural "Abundance," not "Too much":

> . . . There are no banyans, frangipani, nor
>   jack-fruit trees; nor an exotic serpent
> life. Ring lizard and snake-skin for the foot, or crocodile;
>
> but here they've cats, not cobras, to
>   keep down the rats. The diffident
> little newt
>
> with white pin-dots on black horizontal spaced
>   out bands lives here; yet there is nothing that
> ambition can buy or take away.

In this setting "the hero, the student, / the steeple-jack, each in his way, / is at home." The student perceives the presence of the human mean beside the natural in "an elegance of which / the source is not bravado" that characterises the architecture of the town, "the antique / sugar-bowl-shaped summer house of interlacing slats," the church spire and its portico "made modester by white-wash." The imaginative harmony of civilisation and nature in the scene is made doubly telling by the intermingling of human and natural attributes in each other's sphere: the waves are "formal," the pitch of the church spire is "not true" as though it had grown there rather than been built.

I have so far spared the reader any discussion of Miss Moore's use of syllabic verse forms. But this is something that immediately distinguishes her poetry and that embodies and reinforces by technical means our sense of that relationship between freedom and formality which we have already sketched. It is the effect of Miss Moore's syllabic measures which permits Robert Lowell to say, "Marianne Moore is an inventor of a new kind of English poem, one that is able to fix the splendor and variety of prose in very compressed spaces."

Already, before World War I, an interest in syllabic form had spread through American poetry. There was, for example, the work of Adelaide Crapsey domesticating the Japanese tanka and haiku with her invention of the five-lined cinquain. This consisted of lines of two, four, six, eight, and two syllables, as in "Triad":

> These be
> Three silent things:
> The falling snow . . . the hour
> Before the dawn . . . the mouth of one
> Just dead.

"Triad" is conventional stuff beside Miss Moore's syllabics, with their variation of line length and unpredictability of rhythmic pattern. Thus the stanzas of "Melancthon" run to a syllable count of four, six, thirteen, and thirteen, but we are conscious at the same time of their open-endedness, the sense rippling on from one verse to the next:

> . . . the blemishes stand up and shout when the object
> in view was a
> renaissance; shall I say
>   the contrary? The sediment of the river which
>   encrusts my joints, makes me very grey but I am used
>
> to it, it may
> remain there; do away
>   with it and I am myself done away with. . . .

Here, we have a rhyme scheme, also reinforced by syllabic count, which compels us to pick out and pronounce "a" so that it chimes with "say" and also to give the kind of attention to "it may / remain there" that we give to Donne's "he that will / Reach her. . . ." We are, among other details, made by the syllabic lay-out to take cognizance of the humbler components of language, the "to it" and the "with it."

In "The Hero" the very uncertainty of the hero's quest is caught up into the irregularly patterned syllabics:

> We do not like some things, and the hero
>   doesn't; deviating head-stones
>   and uncertainty;
>   going where one does not wish
>   to go; suffering and not
>   saying so; standing and listening where something
>   is hiding. The hero shrinks
> as what it is flies out on muffled wings, with twin yellow
>   eyes—to and fro—

The full effect of this uncertainty of count—an uncertainty without limpness, with imaginative pressure behind it—depends on a foil throughout the poem created by rhyming the first line of each stanza with the last two on the sound "o." Thus "so" and "grow" in the last two lines of verse one are taken up by "hero" in verse two (quoted above) and re-echoed by "yellow" and "to and fro" at the end, a device repeated in all six stanzas. Here an unexpected placing of rhyme words works together with the syllabification to produce a curious ebbing away from known to unknown and a final return.

The effects of Marianne Moore's syllabics and her rhyming has been well described by Robert Beloof in an article that has received little attention, namely his "Prosody and Tone," reprinted below (pp. 144–49). There, the whole aim is to examine the interaction of these two, prosody and tone, and Beloof sees her syllabic technique as principally tending "to minimize the sense of metric regularity." He sums up:

> The sparseness of rhyme sets, the redoubling of the sense of run-on line by ending lines with unimportant words or hyphenations, the leaping between somewhat extreme lengths of line—these are all devices to minimize a firm sense of line as a rhythmic unit. The basic rhythmic power and beauty exploited by syllabic poetry lies traditionally in this firm sense of length of line which becomes a rhythmic unit used contrapuntally against the rhythm of the phrase. She uses this contrapuntal technique to a degree, but it is minimized. Her manipulation of syllabic prosody makes a somewhat unique contribution to the historic use of this form in the devices by which, as we have described, she accomplishes this minimization.

The minimization of which Mr. Beloof speaks is illustrated at the beginning of "Virginia Britannia," where the swaying and leisurely rhythmic effect prepares us for a poem with that "true sauntering eye" Thoreau asks for, going from shore, to churchyard, to tomb:

> Pale sand edges England's Old
> Dominion. The air is soft, warm, hot
> above the cedar-dotted emerald shore
> known to the red bird, the red-coated musketeer,
> the trumpet-flower, the cavalier,
> the parson, and the wild parishoner. A deer-
> track in a church-floor
> brick, and a fine pavement tomb with engraved top, remain.
> The now tremendous vine-encompassed hackberry
> starred with the ivy-flower,
> shades the church tower;
> And a great sinner lyeth here under the sycamore.

Mr. Beloof concludes, and rightly if we bear the above quotation in mind, that the syllabic poetry of Miss Moore "is made to *sound* very much like her free verse poems . . ."—like, that is to say, "Marriage," "Silence," "A Grave." His remarks go a long way toward explaining the characteristic feel of Miss Moore's verse and the source of her originality. This originality is, at the same time, a question of content and also an extending of tradition. If she is "an inventor of a new kind of English poem . . . able to fix the splendor and variety of prose statement in very compressed spaces," she does, in her own way, what has long appealed to poets—namely, makes available to verse the materials and cadences of prose speech and prose writing. Chaucer did it. Wyatt did it. Miss Moore does it with the speech and writing of her own day. Her raids on prose are as audacious as theirs, and perhaps more so when she insists, "nor is it valid / to discriminate against 'business documents and / school books'; all these phenomena are important." Thus "Silence" consists of two extended prose quotations—one from a Miss A. M. Holmans' recollections of her father, the other from Prior's life of Edmund Burke. "Four Quartz Crystal Clocks" transpired from a foray into a leaflet, *The World's Most Accurate Clocks,* put out by the Bell Telephone Company, but one would never mistake the result for anything other than Miss Moore, as fact is scrutinised by those "sharpened faculties which require exactness" which she has admired in another poet; "we know," she says:

> . . . that a quartz prism when
> the temperature changes, feels
>   the change and that the then
> electrified alternate edges
>   oppositely charged, threaten
>   careful timing; so that
> this water-clear crystal as the Greeks used to say,
>   this 'clear ice' must be kept at the
> same coolness. Repetition, with
>   the scientist, should be
> synonymous with accuracy. . . .

After the scientist, we move in this poem to the lemur student, the aye-aye, angwan-tibo, potto and loris. Indeed, we never quite know where we are going to in one of Miss Moore's pieces, nor where the next leap will take us. If she respects "logic employed to ends that are disinterested," hers is a logic scarcely foreseeable or linear. In this she is at one with that interest in "the intersection of loci" common to Pound, Eliot, and Williams. Thus Williams, who approved of "Marriage" as "an anthology of transit," could describe his own poems as "rigamaroles." The word would happily describe many a Moore poem, as would his formulation of what a poem is and does: it is "tough . . . from the attenuated power which draws perhaps many broken things into a dance by giving them thus a full being."

In "Marriage," the dance of broken things—the fragments of omnivorous reading and looking rather than the urban detritus of Williams—can comprise a phrase from a review of Santayana's poems (". . . something feline . . . something colubrine. . . .") in the *New Republic,* a memory of a Persian miniature, cymbal music, a quotation on waterfalls:

> And he has beauty also;
> it's distressing—the O thou
> to whom from whom,
> without whom nothing—Adam;

'something feline,
something colubrine'—how true!
a crouching mythological monster
in that Persian miniature of emerald mines,
raw silk—ivory white, snow white,
oyster white and six others—
that paddock full of leopards and giraffes—
long lemon-yellow bodies
sown with trapezoids of blue.
Alive with words,
vibrating like a cymbal
touched before it has been struck,
he has prophesied correctly—
the industrious waterfall,
'the speedy stream
which violently bears all before it,
at one time silent as the air
and now as powerful as the wind'.

Half the pleasure of the poems lies in their "anthology of transit," in the way we are conducted irresistibly in, say, "Then the ermine," from the Duke of Beaufort's motto, through Lavater's physiography, and finally to violets by Dürer; or, in "Tom Fool at Jamaica," in the way prophet, schoolboy, and Victor Hugo all serve as prelude to a rhapsody on a race-horse:

Look at Jonah embarking for Joppa, deterred by
the whale; hard going for a statesman whom nothing could detain
although one who would not rather die than repent.
Be infallible at your peril, for your system will fail,
and select as a model the schoolboy in Spain
who at the age of six, portrayed a mule and jockey
who had pulled up for a snail.

"There is a submerged magnificence, as Victor Hugo
said." *Sentir avec ardeur;* that's it. . . .

In "Marriage" and also in "The Octopus"—a poem from the same phase which presses into service The National Parks Portfolio, details of Greek philosophy, not to mention an item from a list of useful inventions (i.e., glass that will bend)—the broken things, assembled into the dance of the whole, work with a power that is often centrifugal and recalls the apparent disconnections of those "chains of incontravertibly logical non-sequiturs" which Miss Moore finds in Williams, thus returning him the compliment in her essay on him in *Predilections*. A new unity, won from the apparently intractable, is a measure of the creative force that permeates these poems of hers where originality and freedom stand on the other side of the equation from decorousness and rectitude. Her best poems are the resolutions of a tough moral elegance. If she is self-reliant like the cat, her self-reliance is outward-going like her interest in detail. Her morality, like her technique, is put on its mettle by facing difficulties imaginatively.

II

Critical writings about the work of Miss Moore fall into two sharp divisions: clear-minded essays—Eliot and Kenner are cases in point—where an exact perception of what she is about eschews all floridness; and, on the other hand, a host of "tributes" in which the poet is reduced to the status of a kind of national pet and where the intellectual stamina finds no answering attitude in the appreciator but calls forth instead sentimental rhapsodizing. One of the more depressing thoughts to cross the mind of anybody who has read such criticism in bulk is to wonder whether Marianne Moore has not suffered more from lax adulation than almost any other significant poet of our century. Perhaps the reason for this lies as much in the nature of the work as in the nature of Miss Moore's more indulgent public. This work is morally "armoured," like some of her favourite animals, but suppose that armor should come to seem quaint, a carapace of knowing quiddities? This is the way many people have apparently read it, and this is the basis for Miss Moore's popular success. Thus the one potential defect in a brilliant oeuvre passes for its virtue in a body of critical writing that seldom engages with the reality.

Robert Duncan, in his "Ideas of the Meaning of Form," puts the matter keenly when, speaking of the type of poem which has earned Miss Moore a wide public in the pages of *The New Yorker*, he writes:

> These poems were practices meant to insure habitual virtues. Vision and flight of the imagination was sacrificed to survival in terms of personal signature. . . . What had been boney insistences and quirks of protective structure now become social gestures of fuss and lapse, a protest of charming helplessness.[4]

Duncan instances "Hometown Piece for Messrs. Alston and Reese," "Enough," and "In the Public Garden" as illustrations of a sacrifice of "character to the possibilities of what America loves in public personality." One could also perhaps trace the limitation in Miss Moore's style back to poems like "Propriety," first gathered into the

[4] *Kulchur*, No. 4 (1961), p. 68.

Collected Poems of 1951, where the effect of spontaneity is consciously worked out and there is a resultant lack of significance in the form of what is offered:

> Some such word
> 　　as the chord
> 　　　　Brahms had heard
> 　　　　from a bird,
> sung down near the root of the throat;
> it's the little downy woodpecker
> 　　　　　　　　spiralling a tree—
> 　　　　　　　　up up up like mercury. . . .

The effect here is to simplify and to sentimentalize. Stylistically it represents a kind of self-parody:

> . . . Brahms and Bach,
> 　　no; Bach and Brahms. To thank Bach
>
> for his song
> first, is wrong.
> 　　　　　　Pardon me; . . . .

The order and the spontaneity no longer coalesce: the order becomes merely typographical dexterity and the spontaneity the exploitation of a willed simplicity. "Propriety" illustrates a loss of stylistic decorum within Miss Moore's chosen limits. Two other much longer poems, "In Distrust of Merits" and "Keeping Their World Large," show what happens when she ventures outside of them. Both attempt to deal with the theme of war, and both fail because the feeling is no longer contained. Her characteristic and remarkable achievements derive from an impersonality in the means of the poetry which, in fact, permits the fusion of both personal and impersonal in their most significant form. There occurs no invitation to "feeling" because the means do not admit of such. In her two wartime pieces, however, the means admit of little else:

> They're fighting, fighting, fighting the blind
> 　　man who thinks he sees—
> who cannot see that the enslaver is
> enslaved; the hater, harmed. O shining O
> 　　　　firm star, O tumultuous
> 　　　　　　　ocean lashed till small things go
> 　　　　as they will, the mountainous
> 　　　　　　　wave makes us who look, know
>
> depth.

It is precisely in the avoidance of an over-elaboration of the rhetorical machinery and of an inviting coyness of diction that makes for the unwavering balance of her finest work. In the less admirable poems, the coyness, as in "Propriety," and the public rhetoric, as in the above quotation from "In Distrust of Merits," seem to have struck a bargain satisfactory to both, yet disconcerting to the reader.

One pauses to register the nature of the defect because an anomaly arising from it has too often gone unnoticed: here is a poet whose public image is now perhaps only slightly less famous than that of Allen Ginsberg, but whose most characteristic and sound work would, from all appearances, have ensured a long and healthy unpopularity. Pound saw in the verse, in 1919, "an arid clarity," certainly not something that would have recommended it to the bosom of a nation, and he described it, unexpectedly, as bordering on despair. Eliot, when he introduced her poems in 1935, recognised that her originality represented qualities not generally assimilable, that her "feeling in one's own way" would be mistaken for frigidity. Thirty years later it is precisely "humanity," "warmth," "delightfulness" that are attributed to these poems, the charge of frigidity having vanished beneath the weight of approval. The true standard of Miss Moore's excellence and the difficulties which ensue once this singular and apparently self-sufficient talent unbends to make friends with the audience are recalled to us by Mr. Kenner when he writes in "Meditation and Enactment":

> One might sort Miss Moore's poems into those that observe, meditate and enact . . . , the rigorous pattern a dimension of meditation and enactment; those that soliloquize, like "A Grave" or "New York," and have as their center of gravity therefore the speaker's probity and occasional tartness; and those (rather frequent of late) that incite, that set themselves to *exact*, appropriate feelings about something public. For her public occasions Miss Moore seems a little dependent on the newspapers: "Carnegie Hall: Rescued" has her inimitable texture, but the sentiment of the poem is extrinsic to that texture.

In *The Complete Poems of Marianne Moore* we now possess a far more representative selection of the verse than that supplied by *A Marianne Moore Reader,* the book Mr. Kenner had under review. "Omissions are not accidents," Miss Moore notes in this newer volume, but perhaps one might add that it does not quite present us with a *complete* poems: "Melancthon" has been suppressed, "Old Tiger" has never been restored to the canon, "Poetry" has been clipped back from twenty-nine to three lines though retained whole in the appendix. "To a Prize Bird" has reappeared from a long oblivion, while "Talisman," "He Made this Screen," and, more importantly, "Radical" and "Feed Me Also River God" still share it. But *The Complete Poems* remains essential for admirers of Miss

Moore's work—at any rate, until another book of that name honors its own title.

III

In selecting the critics to be included in the present volume, the chief aim was to unite essays that would cover Miss Moore's original verse, her translations, and also her highly idiosyncratic prose writing. Mr. Burke's seems the best available apologia for this last: perhaps, ideally, it should be confronted by Gorham Munson's contrary view in his pioneering essay on Miss Moore in *Destinations* of 1928, where he urges:

> The critic must be ambitious and as Miss Moore is not. She attempts to make no more than a sensitive impressionistic sketch of her reading, a sketch that is always liberally studded with quotations from the author under review, and carries a valuable sentence or two of acute technical understanding for good measure. The quotations are ably selected for the object she has in mind, which is to give the "flavour" of the author. But, after all, the "flavour" is *in* the book and each reader of it may garner his own impressions. The critic must do more than that. At any rate, he should not be backward about handling ideas.

I have omitted Mr. Munson's essay only because other critics have gone over the same ground and viewed it in a wider perspective made possible by the lapse of time.

In the chronological arrangement, going from Pound's early and slightly puzzled note of 1918 through Eliot's review of 1923 and his introduction to the 1935 selection, through Blackmur's weighty study and on to Henry Gifford's placing of Miss Moore vis-à-vis Emily Dickinson, I hope that the unfolding awareness of various aspects over the course of time will communicate itself to the reader in terms of a voyage of discovery. Writing in the early thirties, T. S. Eliot could say: "We know very little about the work of our contemporaries. . . . It may have merits which exist only for contemporary sensibility; it may have concealed virtues which will only become apparent with time." The concealed virtues of Miss Moore's work have surely, by now, become more than apparent: she is a contemporary whose value the passage of the years has made plain and one whom genuine criticism has done much to rescue from the morass of merely good-natured approval.

A Letter to Ezra Pound

from Marianne Moore

14 St. Luke's Place,
New York City,
January 9, 1919.

Dear Mr. Pound:

In your letter of December 16th,[1] I have a great deal to thank you for. My contemporaries are welcome to anything they have come upon first and I do not resent unfriendly criticism, much less that which is friendly.

I am glad to give you personal data and hope that the bare facts that I have to offer, may not cause work that I may do from time to time, utterly to fail in interest. Even if they should, it is but fair that those who speak out, should not lie in ambush. I was born in 1887 and brought up in the home of my grandfather, a clergyman of the Presbyterian church. I am Irish by descent, possibly Scotch also, but purely Celtic, was graduated from Bryn Mawr in 1909 and taught shorthand, typewriting and commercial law at the government Indian School in Carlisle, Pennsylvania, from 1911 until 1915. In 1916, my mother and I left our home in Carlisle to be with my brother—also a clergyman—in Chatham, New Jersey—but since the war, Chaplain of the battleship Rhode Island and by reason of my brother's entering the navy, my mother and I are living at present in New York, in a small apartment. Black Earth,[2] the poem to which I think you refer, was written about an elephant that I have, [*sic*] named Melancthon; and contrary to your impression, I am altogether a blond and have red hair.

The first writing I did was a short story published in 1907 by the Bryn Mawr undergraduate monthly and during 1908 and nine, I

"A Letter to Ezra Pound." Letter from Marianne Moore to Ezra Pound, January 1, 1919. Copyright 1965 by Marianne Moore. Reprinted by permission of the author. Also appears in *Perspectives*, ed. Noel Stock (Chicago: Henry Regnery Co., 1965), pp. 116–20.

[1] *Letters of Ezra Pound*, ed. by D. D. Paige (New York: Harcourt, Brace & Company, 1950). Letter No. 155.

[2] [In *Collected Poems* (1951) this poem appears as *Melancthon*. In *The Complete Poems* (1967) it has been deleted.]

assisted with the editing of the magazine and contributed verse to it.

Any verse that I have written, has been an arrangement of stanzas, each stanza being an exact duplicate of every other stanza. I have occasionally been at pains to make an arrangement of lines and rhymes that I liked, repeat itself, but the form of the original stanza of anything I have written has been a matter of expediency, hit upon as being approximately suitable to the subject. The resemblance of my progress to your beginnings is an accident so far as I can see. I have taken great pleasure in both your prose and your verse, but it is what my mother terms the saucy parts, which have most fixed my attention. In 1911, my mother and I were some months in England and happening into Elkin Mathews's shop, were shown photographs of you which we were much pleased to see. I like a fight but I admit that I have at times objected to your promptness with the cudgels. I say this merely to be honest. I have no Greek, unless a love for it may be taken as a knowledge of it and I have not read very voraciously in French; I do not know Ghil and La Forgue and know of no tangible French influence on my work. Gordon Craig, Henry James, Blake, the minor prophets and Hardy, are so far as I know, the direct influences bearing on my work.

I do not appear. Originally, my work was refused by the Atlantic Monthly and other magazines and recently I have not offered it. My first work to appear outside of college was a poem, which one of three, I do not recall—published by the Egoist in 1915 and shortly afterward, four or five poems of mine were published by Poetry, a fact which pleased me at the time, but one's feeling changes and not long ago when Miss Monroe invited me to contribute, I was not willing to. Alfred Kreymborg has been hospitable and does not now shut the door to me and Miss Anderson has been most kind in sending me copies of a number of The Little Review in which some lines of mine have appeared with which I am wholly dissatisfied. Moreover, I am not heartily in sympathy with the Little Review though I have supported other magazines for which less could be said. I grow less and less desirous of being published, produce less and have a strong feeling for letting alone what little I do produce. My work jerks and rears and I cannot get up enthusiasm for embalming what I myself, accept conditionally.

Anything that is a stumbling block to my reader, is a matter of regret to me and punctuation ought to be exact. Under ordinary circumstances, it is as great a hardship to me to be obliged to alter punctuation as to alter words, though I will admit that at times I am heady and irresponsible.

I like New York, the little quiet part of it in which my mother and I live. I like to see the tops of the masts from our door and to go to the wharf and look at the craft on the river.

I do not feel that anything phenomenal is to be expected of New York and I sometimes feel as if there are too many captains in one boat, but on the whole, the amount of steady co-operation that is to be counted on in the interest of getting things launched, is an amazement to me. I am interested to know of your having had a hand in the publishing of T. S. Eliot. I like his work. Over here, it strikes me that there is more evidence of power among painters and sculptors than among writers.

I am glad to have you send the prose to the Egoist and to have you keep the two poems that you have, for your quarterly. As soon as I have it, I shall send you something new. Perhaps you would be interested in seeing a poem which I have just given to one of our new magazines here, a proposed experiment under the direction of Maxwell Bodenheim, and a poem of mine which appeared in the Bryn Mawr college Lantern last year?

To capitalize the first word of every line, is rather slavish and I have substituted small letters for capitals in the enclosed versions of the two poems you have.

I fully agree with you in what you say about the need of being more than defensible when giving offense. I have made

> You are right, that swiftmoving sternly
> Intentioned swayback baboon is nothing
> to you and the chimpanzee?

to read

> You are right about it; that wary,
> Presumptuous young baboon is nothing to
> you and the chimpanzee?

For

> And the description is finished. Of the jaguar with the
> pneumatic Feet.

read

> What is there to look at? And of the leopard, spotted
> underneath and on its toes:

Leopards are not spotted underneath, but in old illuminations they are, and on Indian printed muslins, and I like the idea that they are.

its-self may read *its self*

and I have made

> The little dish, dirt brown, mulberry

> White, powder blue or oceanic green—is half human
> and any
>   Thing peacock is "divine."

to read

> the little dishes, brown, mulberry
> or sea green are half human and waiving the matter of
> artistry,
>   anything which can not be reproduced, is "divine." [3]

Confusion is created by introducing contradictory references to lizards;
I have therefore left out stanzas seven and eight and I have made
other alterations.

In *A Graveyard*,[4] I have made *is* to end the line as you suggest and
for the sake of symmetry, have altered the arrangement of lines in
the preceding stanzas. I realize that by writing consciousness and
volition, emphasis is obtained which is sacrificed by retaining the order
which I have, and I am willing to make the change, though I prefer
the original order.

Sincerely yours,
Marianne Moore

[3] [All these quotations are from "Old Tiger," a poem not admitted to either
Collected Poems or *Complete Poems*.]

[4] [Later entitled "A Grave."]

The Art of Poetry: Marianne Moore

An Interview with Donald Hall

American poetry is a great literature, and it has only come to its maturity in the last forty years; Walt Whitman and Emily Dickinson in the last century were rare examples of genius isolated in a hostile environment. One decade gave America the major figures of our modern poetry: Wallace Stevens was born in 1879, and T. S. Eliot in 1888. To the ten years which these dates enclose belong H. D., Robinson Jeffers, John Crowe Ransom, William Carlos Williams, Ezra Pound and Marianne Moore.

Marianne Moore, surely the leading woman in modern American literature, began to publish during the First World war. She was printed and praised in Europe by the expatriates T. S. Eliot and Ezra Pound. In Chicago Harriet Monroe's magazine *Poetry,* which provided the enduring showcase for the new poetry, published her too. But she was mainly a poet of New York, of the Greenwich Village group which created magazines called *Others* and *Broom.* The poets with whom she was mostly associated were Alfred Kreymbourg, William Carlos Williams and Wallace Stevens—Stateside representatives of the miraculous generation.

Marianne Moore has settled not in Bloomsbury or Rapallo but in Brooklyn. She moved there from the Village in 1929, into the apartment house where she still lives.[1] To visit her you cross Brooklyn Bridge, turn left at Myrtle Avenue, follow the elevated for a mile or two, and then turn right onto her street. It is pleasantly lined with a few trees, and Miss Moore's apartment is conveniently near a grocery store and the Presbyterian church which she attends.

The interview took place in November 1960, the day before the election. The front door of Miss Moore's apartment opens onto a long

[1] [This was written before Miss Moore's return to Manhattan.]

narrow corridor. Rooms lead off to the right, and at the end of the corridor is a large sitting room which overlooks the street. On top of a bookcase which ran the length of the corridor was a Nixon button.

Miss Moore and the interviewer sat in her sitting room, a microphone between them. Piles of books stood everywhere. On the walls hung a variety of paintings. One came from Mexico, a gift of Mabel Dodge; others were examples of the heavy, tea-colored oils which Americans hung in the years before 1914. The furniture was old-fashioned and dark.

Miss Moore spoke with an accustomed scrupulosity, and with a humor which her readers will recognize. When she ended a sentence with a phrase which was particularly telling, or even tart, she glanced quickly at the interviewer to see if he was amused, and then snickered gently. Later Miss Moore took the interviewer to an admirable lunch at a nearby restaurant. She decided not to wear her Nixon button because it clashed with her coat and hat.

Interviewer

I understand that you were born in St. Louis only about ten months before T. S. Eliot. Did your families know each other?

Moore

No, we did not know the Eliots. We lived in Kirkwood, Missouri, where my grandfather was pastor of the First Presbyterian Church. T. S. Eliot's grandfather—Dr. William Eliot—was a Unitarian. We left when I was about seven, my grandfather having died in 1894, February 20th. My grandfather like Dr. Eliot had attended ministerial meetings in St. Louis. Also, at stated intervals, various ministers met for luncheon. After one of these luncheons my grandfather said, "When Dr. William Eliot asks the blessing and says, 'and this we ask in the name of our Lord Jesus Christ,' he is Trinitarian enough for me." The Mary Institute, for girls, was endowed by him as a memorial to his daughter Mary, who had died.

Interviewer

How old were you when you started to write poems?

Moore

Well, let me see, in Bryn Mawr, I think. I was eighteen when I
entered Bryn Mawr. I was born in 1887, I entered college in 1906.
Now how old would I have been? Can you deduce my probable age?

Interviewer

Eighteen or nineteen.

Moore

I had no literary plans, but I was interested in the undergraduate
monthly magazine, and to my surprise I wrote one or two little things
for it and the editors elected me to the board. It was my sophomore
year, I am sure it was, and I stayed on, I believe. And then when I
had left college I offered contributions (we weren't paid) to *The
Lantern*, the alumnae magazine. But I didn't feel that my product
was anything to shake the world.

Interviewer

At what point did poetry become world-shaking for you?

Moore

Never! . . . I believe I was more interested in painting then. At
least I said so. I remember Mrs. Otis Skinner saying at Commence-
ment time, the year I was graduated, "What would you like to be?"
"A painter," I said.
"Well, I'm not surprised," Mrs. Skinner answered. I had something
on that she liked, some kind of summer dress. She commended it and
said, "Well, I'm not at all surprised."
I like stories. I like fiction. And—this sounds rather pathetic and
bizarre—I think my verse perhaps is the next best thing to it. Didn't
I write something one time, "Part of a Poem, Part of a Novel, Part
of a Play"? I think that was all too truthful. I could visualize scenes,
and deplored the fact that Henry James had to do it unchallenged.
Now if I couldn't write fiction, I'd like to write plays. In fact, the
theatre is the most pleasant, in fact my favorite form of recreation . . .

Interviewer

Do you go often?

Moore

No. Never. Unless someone invites me. Lillian Hellman invited me to *Toys in the Attic,* and I am very happy that she did. I would have had no notion of the vitality of the thing and her skill as a writer, If I hadn't gone to the play. I would like to go again. The accuracy of the vernacular! It's enviable. That's the kind of thing I am interested in. I'm always noting down little local expressions and accents. I think I should be in some philological operation or enterprise. I am so very much interested in dialects and intonations. I don't think any of that comes into my so-called poems at all.

Interviewer

I wonder what Bryn Mawr meant for you as a poet. You write that most of your time there was spent in the biological laboratories. Did you like biology better than literature as a subject for study? Did the training possibly affect your poetry?

Moore

Did laboratory studies affect my poetry? I am sure they did. I found the biology courses—minor, major and histology—exhilarating. I thought, in fact, of studying medicine. Precision, economy of statement, logic employed to ends that are disinterested, drawing and identifying, liberate—at least have some bearing on—the imagination, it seems to me.

Interviewer

Did moving to New York, and the stimulation of the writers you found there lead you to write more poems than you would otherwise have written?

Moore

I'm sure it did—seeing what others wrote, liking this or that. With me it's always some fortuity that traps me. I certainly never intended to write poetry. It never came into my head to think of it. And now, too, I think each time I write that it may be the last time; then something takes my fancy. Everything I have written is the result of reading or of interest in people, I'm sure of that. I had no ambitions to be a writer.

Interviewer

Let me see. You taught at the Carlisle Indian School, after Bryn Mawr. Then after you moved to New York in 1918 you taught at a private school and worked in a library. Did these occupations have anything to do with you as a writer?

Moore

I think they hardened my muscles considerably, my mental approach to things. Working as a librarian was a big help, a tremendous help. Miss Leonard of the Hudson Park branch of the New York Public Library opposite our house came to see me one day. I wasn't in, and she asked my mother if she thought I would care to be on the staff, work in the library, because I was so fond of books and liked to talk about them to people. My mother said no, she thought not; the shoemaker's children never have shoes, I probably would feel if I joined the staff that I had no time to read. When I came home she told me, and I said, "Why, certainly. I'll tell her that would be ideal!" Only I wouldn't work more than half a day. If I had worked all day and maybe evenings or overtime, like the mechanics, why it would not have been ideal.

As a free service we were assigned books to review and I did like that. We didn't get paid but we had the chance to diagnose. I revelled in that. Somewhere I believe I have carbon copies of those "P-slip" summaries. They were the kind of things that brought the worst-best out. I was always wondering why they didn't honor me with an art book or medical book or even a history, or criticism. But no, it was fiction, silent movie fiction.

Interviewer

Did you travel at this time? Did you go to Europe at all?

Moore

In 1911. My mother and I went to England for about two months, July and August probably. We went to Paris and we stayed on the left bank, in a pension on the rue Valette, where Calvin wrote his *Institutes,* I believe. Not far from the Panthéon and the Luxembourg Gardens. I have been quite interested in seeing Sylvia Beach's book, and reading about Ezra Pound and his Paris days. Where was I and what was I doing? I think, with the objective of an evening stroll—it was one of the hottest summers the world has ever known, 1911—we walked along to 12, rue L'Odéon, to see Sylvia Beach's shop. It wouldn't occur to me to say, "Here am I, I'm a writer, would you talk to me awhile?" I had no feeling at all about anything like that. I wanted to observe things. And we went to every museum in Paris, I think, except two.

Interviewer

Have you been back since?

Moore

Not to Paris. Only in England in 1935 or 1936. I like England.

Interviewer

You have mostly stayed put in Brooklyn, then, since you moved here in 1929?

Moore

Except for four trips to the West: Los Angeles, San Francisco, and British Columbia. My mother and I went through the canal previously, to San Francisco, and by rail to Seattle.

Interviewer

Have you missed the Dodgers here, since *they* went West?

Moore

Very much and I am told that they miss us.

Interviewer

I am still interested in those early years in New York. William Carlos Williams, in his *Autobiography,* says that you were "a rafter holding up the superstructure of our uncompleted building," when he talks about the Greenwich Village group of writers. I guess these were people who contributed to *Others.*

Moore

I never was a rafter holding up anyone! I have his *Autobiography* and took him to task for his misinformed statements about Robert McAlmon and Bryher. In my indignation I missed some things I ought to have seen.

Interviewer

To what extent did the *Others* contributors form a group?

Moore

We did forgather quite a little. Alfred Kreymbourg was editor, and was married to Gertrude Lord at the time, one of the loveliest persons I have ever met. And they had a little apartment somewhere in the Village. There was considerable unanimity about that group.

Interviewer

Someone called Alfred Kreymbourg your American discoverer. Do you suppose this is true?

Moore

Perhaps it *could* be said; he did all he could to promote me. Miss Monroe and the Aldingtons had asked me simultaneously to contribute to *Poetry* and *The Egoist* in 1917, practically at the same time. Alfred Kreymbourg was not inhibited. I was a little different from the others. He thought I might pass as a novelty, I guess.

Interviewer

What was your reaction when H.D. and Bryher brought out your first collection, which they called *Poems,* in 1921 without your knowledge? Why had you delayed to do it yourself?

Moore

To issue my slight product—conspicuously tentative—seemed to me premature. I disliked the term "poetry" for any but Chaucer's or Shakespeare's or Dante's. I no longer feel my original instinctive hostility to the word, since it's a convenient, almost unavoidable term for the thing—although hardly for me:—my observations, experiments in rhythm, or exercises in composition. What I write, as I have said before, could only be called poetry because there is no other category in which to put it. For the chivalry of the undertaking—issuing my verse for me in 1921, certainly in format choicer than in content—I am intensely grateful. Again, in 1925, it seemed to me not very judicious of Faber and Faber, and simultaneously of the Macmillan Company, to propose a *Selected Poems* for me. Desultory occasional magazine publications seemed to me sufficient and plenty conspicuous.

Interviewer

Had you been sending poems to magazines before *The Egoist* printed your first poem?

Moore

I must have. I have a little curio, a little wee book about 2″ by 3″, or 2½″, by 3″, in which I systematically entered everything sent out, when I got it back, if they took it, and how much I got for it. That lasted about a year, I think. I can't care as much as all that. I don't know that I submitted anything that wasn't extorted from me.

I have at present three onerous tasks, and one interferes with the other, and I don't know how I am going to write anything. If I get a promising idea I set it down, and let it stay there. I don't make myself do anything with it. I've had several things in *The New Yorker*. And I said to them, "I might never write again," and not to expect me to. Oh, I never knew anyone who had a passion for words who had as much difficulty in saying things as I do. I very seldom say them in a manner I like. If I do it's because I don't know I'm trying. I've written several things for *The New Yorker*—and I did want to write them.

Interviewer

When did you last write a poem?

Moore

It appeared in August. What was it about? Oh, . . . Carnegie Hall. You see, anything that really rouses me . . .

Interviewer

How does a poem start for you?

Moore

A felicitous phrase springs to mind—or a word or two, say—simultaneous usually with some thought or object of equal attraction: "Its leaps should be *set* / to the flageo*let*": "Kattydid-wing subdivided by *sun* / till the nettings are *legion*." I like light rhymes, inconspicuous rhymes and unpompous conspicuous rhymes: Gilbert and Sullivan:

> and yet when someone's near
> we manage to appear
> as impervious to fear
> as anybody here.

I have a passion for rhythm and accent, and so blundered into versifying. I consider the stanza the unit, and thus came to hazard hyphens at the end of the line. I found that readers think of the hyphen and are distracted from the content, so I try not to use hyphens.

My interest in La Fontaine originated entirely independent of content. I then fell a prey to that surgical kind of courtesy of his.

> I fear that appearances are worshipped throughout France
> Whereas pre-eminence perchance
> Merely means a pushing person.

I like the unaccented syllable and nearly accented near-rhyme:

> By love and his blindness
> Possibly a service was done,
> Let lovers say. A lonely man has no criterion.

Interviewer

What in your reading of your background led you to write the way you do write? Was imagism a help to you?

Moore

No. I wondered why anyone would adopt the term.

Interviewer

The descriptiveness of your poems has nothing to do with them, you think?

Moore

No; I really don't. I was rather sorry to be a pariah, or at least that I had no connection with anything. But I *did* feel gratitude to *Others.*

Interviewer

Where do you think your style of writing came from? Was it gradual accumulation, out of your character? Or does it have literary antecedents?

Moore

Not so far as I know. Ezra Pound said, "Someone has been reading La Forgue, and French authors." Well, sad to say, I had not read any of them until fairly recently. Retroactively I see that Francis Jammes' titles and treatment are a good deal like my own. I seem almost a plagiarist.

Interviewer

And the extensive use of quotations?

Moore

I was just trying to be honorable and not to steal things. I've always felt that if a thing has been said in the very best way, how can you say it better? If I wanted to say something and somebody had said it ideally, then I'd take it but give the person credit for it. That's all there is to that. If you are charmed by an author, I think it's a very strange and invalid imagination that doesn't love to share it. Somebody else should read it, don't you think?

Interviewer

Did any prose stylists help you in finding your poetic style? Elizabeth Bishop mentions Poe's prose, in connection with your writing, and you have always made people thing of Henry James.

Moore

Prose stylists, very much. Doctor Johnson on Richard Savage:

> He was in two months illegitimated by the Parliament, and disowned by his mother, doomed to poverty and obscurity, and launched upon the ocean of life only that he might be swallowed by its quicksands, or dashed upon its rocks . . . it was his peculiar happiness that he scarcely ever found a stranger whom he did not leave a friend; but it must likewise be added that, he had not often a friend long without obliging him to become a stranger.

Or Edmund Burke on the colonies: "You can shear a wolf; but will he comply?" Or Sir Thomas Browne: "States are not governed by

Ergotisms." He calls a bee, "that industrious flie," and his home, his "hive." His manner is a kind of erudition-proof sweetness. Or Sir Francis Bacon: "Civil war is like the heat of fever; a foreign war is like the heat of exercise." Or Cellini: "I had by me a dog black as a mulberry . . . I swelled up in my rage like an asp." Or Caesar's *Commentaries,* and Zenophon's *Cynegeticus:* the gusto and interest in every detail! In Henry James it is the essays and letters especially that affect me. In Ezra Pound, *The Spirit of Romance:* his definiteness, his indigenously unmistakable accent. Charles Norman says in his biography, *Ezra Pound,* that Pound said to a poet: "nothing, *nothing,* that you couldn't in some circumstance, under stress of some emotion, *actually say.*" And Ezra said of Shakespeare and Dante: "Here we are with the masters; of neither can we say, 'he is the greater'; of each we must say, 'he is unexcelled.' "

Interviewer

Do you have in your own work any favorites and unfavorites?

Moore

Indeed, I do. I think the most difficult thing for me is to be satisfactorily lucid, yet have enough implication in it to suit myself. That's a problem. And I don't approve of my "enigmas," or as somebody said, "the not ungreen grass."

I said to my mother one time, "How did you ever permit me to let this be printed?"

And she said, "You didn't ask my advice."

Interviewer

Do you go for criticism to your family or friends?

Moore

Well, not friends, but my brother if I get a chance. When my mother said, "You didn't ask my advice," must have been years ago, because when I wrote "A Face," I had written something first about "the adder and the child with a bowl of porridge," and she said, "Well, it won't do."

"All right," I said, "but I have to produce something." Cyril Connolly had asked me for something for Horizon. So I wrote "A Face." That is one of the few things I ever set down and it didn't give me any trouble. And she said, "I like it." I remember that.

Then, much before that, I wrote "The Buffalo." I thought it would probably outrage a number of persons because it had to me a kind of pleasing jerky progress. I thought, "Well, if it seems bad my brother will tell me, and if it has any point he'll detect it."

And he said, with a considerable gusto, "It takes my fancy." I was happy as could be.

Interviewer

Did you ever suppress anything because of family objections?

Moore

Yes, "the adder and the child with a bowl of porridge." I never even wanted to improve it.

You know, Mr. Saintsbury said that Andrew Lang wanted him to contribute something on Poe, and he did, and Lang returned it. He said, "Once a thing has been rejected, I never would offer it to the most different of editors." Well, that shocked me. Why I have offered a thing, submitted it thirty-five times. Not simultaneously of course.

Interviewer

A poem?

Moore

Yes. I am very tenacious.

Interviewer

Do people ever ask you to write poems for them?

Moore

Oh, continually. Everything from on the death of a dog to a little item for an album.

Interviewer

Do you ever write them?

Moore

Once when I was in the library we gave a party for Miss Leonard, and I wrote a line or two of doggerel about a bouquet of violets we gave her. It has no life or point. It's inert. It was meant well but it didn't amount to anything. Then in college, I had a sonnet as an assignment. The epitome of weakness.

Interviewer

I'm interested in asking about the principles, and the methods, of your way of writing. What is the rationale behind syllabic verse? How does it differ from free verse in which the line length is controlled visually but not arithmetically?

Moore

It never occurred to me that what I wrote was something to define. I am governed by the pull of the sentence as the pull of a fabric is governed by gravity. I like the end-stopped line and dislike the reversed order of words.

Interviewer

How do you plan the shape of your stanzas? I am thinking of the poems, usually syllabic, which employ a repeated stanza form. Do you ever experiment with shapes before you write, by drawing lines on a page?

Moore

Never, I never "plan" a stanza. Words cluster like chromosomes, determining the procedure. I may influence an arrangement or thin it, then try to have successive stanzas identical with the first. Spontaneous initial originality—say, impetus—seems difficult to reproduce consciously later. As Stravinsky said about pitch: "If I transpose it for some reason, I am in danger of losing the freshness of first contact and will have difficulty in recapturing its attractiveness."

No, I never "draw lines." I make a rhyme conspicuous to me at a glance, by underlining with red, blue, or other pencil—as many colors as I have rhymes to differentiate. However, if the phrases recur in too incoherent an architecture—as print—I notice that the words as a tune do not sound right.

I may start a piece, find it obstructive, lack a way out, and not complete the thing for a year, or years. I am thrifty. I salvage anything promising and set it down in a small notebook.

Interviewer

I wonder if the act of translating La Fontaine's *Fables* helped you as a writer?

Moore

Indeed it did. It was the best help I've ever had. I suffered frustration. I'm so naive, so docile, and I *tend* to take anybody's word for anything the person says, even in matters of art. The publisher who had commissioned the *Fables* died. I had no publisher. Well, I struggled on for a time and it didn't go very well. I thought, well I'll ask if they don't want to terminate the contract. Then I'll offer it elsewhere. I thought Macmillan, who took such an interest in me, would like it. And the editor there in charge of translations said, "Well, I studied French at Cornell, took a degree in French. I love French, and—well, I think I would put it away for a while, about ten years. And besides, it will hurt your own work. You won't be able to write yourself."

"Oh," I said, "that's one reason I was undertaking it. I thought it would train me, assist me, give me incentive."

"Oh no, you won't be able to write anything of your own."

I was most dejected by this, and said, "Tell me what's wrong? Are the meanings not sound or the rhythms?"

"Well, there are conflicts." And the editor reiterated, many times, "There are conflicts." And I yet don't know what they are or were. A little editorial, I think.

I said, "Don't write me a letter extenuating the return of them. Just send the material in the envelope I put with it." I had submitted it in January and this was May. And I had had a kind of uneasy hope that all would be well. Meanwhile I had volumes, hours, and years of work yet to do and I might as well go on and do it, I had thought. To have this ultimatum was devastating.

At the same time Monroe Engle of the Viking Press wrote to me and said that he had supposed I had a commitment for my *Fables*, but if I hadn't would I let the Viking Press see them? I feel an everlasting gratitude to him.

However I said, "I can't offer you something when somebody else thinks it isn't fit to print. I would have to have someone to stabilize it and guarantee that the meanings are sound."

And Mr. Engle said, "Who do you think could do that? Whom would you like?"

And I said, "Well, Harry Levin," because he had written a very shrewd review of Edna St. Vincent Millay's and George Dillon's translation of Baudelaire. I admired the finesse of that review.

Mr. Engle said, "I'll ask him. But you won't hear for a long time. He's very busy. And how much do you think we ought to offer him?"

"Well," I said, "not less than ten dollars a book, and there wouldn't be any incentive in it, to undertake the bother of it, if he weren't given twenty."

"Oh," he said, "that will reduce your royalties, supposing we gave you an advance."

I said, "I don't want an advance, I don't want even to consider it."

"Well," he said, "that is like you."

And then Harry Levin said, right away, that he would be glad to do it as a refreshment against the chores of the term. It was a very dubious refreshment, let me tell you. He is precise without being abusive, and did not "resign."

Interviewer

I've been asking you about your poems, which is of course what interests me most. But you were editor of the *Dial*, too, and I want to ask you a few things about that. You were editor from 1926 until it ended in 1929, I think. How did you first come to be associated with it?

Moore

Let me see. I think I took the initiative, I sent the editors a couple of things and they sent them back. And Lola Ridge had a party—she had a large apartment on a ground floor somewhere—and John Reed and Marsden Hartley, who was very confident with the brush, and Scofield Thayer, editor of the *Dial,* were there. And much to my disgust, we were induced to read something we had written. And Scofield Thayer said of my piece, "Would you send that to us at the Dial?"

"I did send it," I said.

And he said, "Well, send it again." That's how it began, I think. Then he said, one time, "I'd like you to meet my partner, Sibley Watson," and I invited him to tea at 152 W. 13th St. I thought Dr. Watson very deep—rare. He said nothing but what he did say was striking and the significance would creep over you as being extremely unanticipated. And they asked me to join the staff at *The Dial.*

Interviewer

I have just been looking at that magazine, the years when you edited it. It's an incredible magazine.

Moore

The Dial? There were some good things in it, weren't there?

Interviewer

Yes. It combined George Saintsbury and Ezra Pound in the same issue. How do you account for it? What made it so good?

Moore

Lack of fear, for one thing. We didn't care what other people said. I never knew a magazine which was so self-propulsive. Everybody liked what he was doing, and if we made grievous mistakes we were sorry but we laughed over them.

Interviewer

Louise Bogan said that *The Dial* made clear "the obvious division between American *avant-garde* and American conventional writing." Do you think this kind of division continues or has continued? Was this in any way a deliberate policy?

Moore

I think that individuality was the great thing. We were not conforming to anything. We certainly didn't have a policy, except I remember hearing the word "intensity" very often. A thing must have an "intensity." That seemed to be the criterion.

The thing applied to it, I think, that should apply to your own writing. As George Grosz said, at that last meeting he attended at the National Institute, "How did I come to be an artist? Endless curiosity, observation, research—and a great amount of joy in the thing." It was a matter of taking a liking to things. Things that were in accordance with your taste. I think that was it. And we didn't care how unhomogeneous they might seem. And didn't Aristotle say that it is the mark of a poet to see resemblances between apparently incongruous things! There was any amount of incentive about it.

Interviewer

Do you think there is anything in the change of literary life in America that would make the *Dial* different if it existed today under the same editors? Were there any special conditions in the twenties that made the literary life of America different?

Moore

I think it is always about the same.

Interviewer

I wonder if it had survived into the thirties if it might have made that rather dry literary decade a little better?

Moore

I certainly think so. Because we weren't in captivity to anything.

Interviewer

Was it just finances that made it stop?

Moore

No, it wasn't the depression at all. No, the conditions changed. Scofield Thayer had a nervous breakdown, and he didn't come to meetings. Sibley Watson was interested in photography and he had a medical degree, is a doctor of medicine, and lived in Rochester. I was alone. I didn't know that Rochester was about a night's journey away and I would say to Dr. Watson, "Couldn't you come for a make-up meeting, or send me these manuscripts and say what you think of them?" I may, as usual, have exaggerated my enslavement and my preoccupation with tasks—writing letters and reading manuscripts. Originally I had said I would come if I didn't have to write letters and didn't have to see contributors. And presently I was doing both. I think it was largely chivalry—the decision to discontinue *The Dial*—because I didn't have time for my own work.

Interviewer

I wonder how you worked as an editor. Hart Crane complains, in one of his letters, that you rearranged "The Wine Menagerie," and changed the title. Do you feel that you were justified? Did you ask for revisions from many poets?

Moore

No. We had an unflexible rule: do not ask changes of so much as a comma. Accept it or reject it. But I felt that in compassion, I must disregard the rule. Hart Crane complains of me? Well, I complain of *him*. He liked the *Dial* and we liked him—friends, and with certain tastes in common. He was in dire need of money. It seemed careless not to so much as ask if he might like to make some changes ("like" in quotation). His gratitude was ardent and later his repudiation of it commensurate—he perhaps being in both instances under a disability with which I was not familiar. (Penalizing us for compassion?) I say "us," and should say "me." Really I am not used to having people in that bemused state. He was so *anxious* to have us take that thing, and so *delighted*. "Well, if you would modify it a little," I said, "we would like it better." Well, I never attended his wild parties. It was lawless of me to suggest changes.

Interviewer

Have you had editors suggest changes to you? Changes in your own poems, I mean?

Moore

No, but my ardor to be helped being sincere, I sometimes *induce* assistance: the *Times,* the *Herald Tribune, The New Yorker,* have a number of times had to patch and piece me out. If you have a genius of an editor, you are blessed: e.g., T. S. Eliot and Ezra Pound, Harry Levin, and others; Irita Van Doren and Miss Belle Rosenbaum.

Have I found "help" helpful? I certainly have; and in three instances when I was at *The Dial,* I hazarded suggestions the results of which to me were drama. Excoriated by George Haven Sheffauer for offering to submit a verbal change or two in his translation of Thomas Mann's *Disorder and Early Sorrow,* I must have posted the suggestions before I was able to withdraw them. In any case, his joyous subsequent retraction of abuse, and his pleasure in the narrative, were not unwelcome. Gilbert Seldes strongly commended me for excisions proposed by me in his "Jonathan Edwards" (for *The Dial*); and I have not ceased to marvel at the overrating by Mark Van Doren of editorial conscience on my reverting (after an interval) to keep something I had wished he would omit. (Verse! but not a sonnet.)

We should try to judge the work of others by the most that it is, and our own if not by the least that it is, should take the least into consideration. I feel that I would not be worth a button if not grateful to be preserved from myself, and informed if what I have written is not to the point. I think we should feel free, like La Fontaine's captious critic, to say, "Your phrases are too long, and the content is not good. Break up the type and put it in the font." As Kenneth Burke says in *Counter-Statement*: "(Great) artists feel as opportunity what others feel as a menace. This ability does not, I believe, derive from exceptional strength, it probably arrives as purely from professional interest the artist may take in his difficulties."

Lew Sarett says, in the *Poetry Society Bulletin,* that we ask of a poet: Does this mean something? Does the poet say what he has to say and in his own manner? Does it stir the reader?

Shouldn't we replace vanity with honesty as Robert Frost recommends? Annoyances abound. We should not find them lethal, a baffled printer's emendations for instance (my "elephant with frog-colored skin" instead of "fog-colored skin," and "the power of the invisible is the invisible," instead of "the power of the visible is the invisible") sounding like a parody on my meticulousness.

Interviewer

Editing the *Dial* must have acquainted you with the writers of the day whom you did not know already. Had you known Hart Crane earlier?

Moore

You remember *Broom*? Well, at the beginning of that magazine, in 1921, Lola Ridge was very hospitable, and she invited Kay Boyle and her husband, a French soldier, and Hart Crane and Elinor Wylie, and some others. I took a great liking to Hart Crane, previous to my work at *The Dial.* We talked about French bindings, and he was so diffident and modest and seemed to have so much intuition, such a feel for things, for books—really a bibliophile—that I took special interest in him. And Doctor Watson and Scofield Thayer liked him ever so much, and felt that he was one of our talents, that he couldn't fit himself into an IBM position to find a livelihood; that we ought to, whenever we could, take anything.

I knew a cousin of his, too, Joe Novak, who is rather proud of him. He lives here in Brooklyn, and is at the Dry Docks Savings Bank and used to work in antiques. Joe was very convinced of Hart's sincerity and his innate love of all that I specified. Anyhow, *The Bridge* is a grand theme. Here and there I think he could have firmed it up. I think it is a terrible thing when a writer is unable to be hard on himself.

Interviewer

Did Crane have anything to do with *Others*?

Moore

Others antedated *Broom. Others* was Alfred Kreymbourg and Skip-
with Connell, Wallace Stevens, William Carlos Williams. Wallace
Stevens—odd; I came very near to meeting him about a dozen times
but I did not meet him till 1941 at Mount Holyoke. It was at the
college's *Entretiens de Pontigny* of which Professor Gustav Cohen
was Chairman. Wallace Stevens was Henry Church's favorite American poet. Mr. Church had published him and some others and me in
Mésure, in Paris. Raymond Queneau translated us.

At the French program at Mount Holyoke one afternoon Wallace
Stevens had a discourse, the one about Goethe dancing on a packet-
boat in black wool stockings. My mother and I were there; and I
gave a reading with commentary. Henry Church had an astoundingly
beautiful Panama hat—a sort of pork-pie with a wide brim, a little
like Bernard Berenson's hats. I have never seen as fine a weave, and
he had a pepper and salt shawl which he draped about himself. The
meeting was on the lawn.

Wallace Stevens was extremely friendly. I think I should have had
a tape recorder on that occasion, for at lunch they seated us all at a
kind of refectory table and there was a girl who kept asking him
questions such as: "Mr. Stevens, have you read "The-Four-Quartets"?

"Yes, I have, but I can't read much of Eliot or I wouldn't have any
individuality of my own."

Interviewer

Do you read new poetry now? Do you try to keep up?

Moore

More or less. I make no effort, and I get something every day. Some
of it is good. But it does interfere with my own tasks. I can't get
much done. Yet I would be a monster if I tossed everything away
without looking at it. And after all I can write more things inside of
half an hour—more notes, letters, cards—then you can think probable.

Interviewer

When you first read Pound in 1916, did you recognize him as one of
the great ones?

Moore

Yes, indeed. That *Spirit of Romance*. I don't think anybody could read that book and feel that a flounderer was writing.

Interviewer

What about the early poems?

Moore

Oh, yes. They seemed a little didactic, but I liked them.

Interviewer

I wanted to ask you a few questions about poetry in general. Somewhere you have said that originality is a by-product of sincerity. You often use moral terms in your criticism. Is the necessary morality specifically literary, a moral use of words, or is it larger? In what way must a man be good if he is to write good poems?

Moore

If emotion is strong, the words are forthright and unambiguous. Someone asked Robert Frost (is this right?) if he was selective. He said, "Call it passionate preference."

Must a man be good to write good poems? The villains in Shakespeare are not illiterate, are they? But rectitude *has* a ring that is implicative, I would say. And with *no* integrity, a man is not likely to write the kind of book I read.

Interviewer

Eliot, in his introduction to your *Selected Poems,* talks about your function as poet relative to the living language, as he calls it. Do you agree that this is a function of a poet? How does the poetry have the effect on the living language? What's the mechanics of it?

Moore

You accept certain modes of saying a thing. It's a fly in amber, as it were, isn't it? Or you strongly repudiate things. You do something of your own, you modify. I think there's no doubt about that.

Interviewer

I want to ask you a question about your correspondence with the Ford Motor Company, those letters which were printed in *The New Yorker*. They were looking for a name for the car they eventually called the Edsel, and they asked you to think of a name that would make people admire the car—

Moore

Elegance and grace, they said it would have—

Interviewer

". . . some visceral feeling of elegance, fleetness, advanced features and design. A name, in short, which flashes a dramatically desirable picture in people's minds."

Moore

Really?

Interviewer

That's what they said, in their first letter to you. I was thinking about this in connection with my question about language. Do you remember Pound's talk about expression and meaning? He says that when expression and meaning are far apart, the culture is in a bad way. I was wondering if this request doesn't ask you to remove expression a bit further from meaning.

Moore

No, I don't think so. At least, exposit the irresistableness of the car. I got deep in motors and turbines and recessed wheels. No. That seemed to me a very worthy pursuit. I was more interested in the mechanics. I am very interested in mechanical things, in mechanics in general. And I enjoyed that assignment, for all it was abortive.

Mr. Pick at the Marquette University procured a young demonstrator of the Edsel to call for me in a black Edsel, to convey me to the auditorium. Nothing was wrong with that Edsel! I thought it was a very handsome car. It came out the wrong year.

Interviewer

Another thing: in your criticism you make frequent analogies between the poet and the scientist. Do you think this analogy is helpful to the modern poet? Most people would consider the comparison a paradox, and assume that the poet and the scientist are opposed.

Moore

Do the poet and the scientist not work analogously? They are willing to waste effort. To be hard on himself is one of the greatest strengths of each. Each is attentive to clues, each must narrow the choice, must strive for precision. As George Grosz says, "In art there is no place for gossip and but a small place for the satirists." The objective is substance. Is it not? Bronowski says in the new *Post* that science is not a mere collection of discoveries, but that science is the process of discovering. In any case it's not a thing established once and for all, it's evolving.

Interviewer

One last question. I was intrigued when you wrote that "America has in Wallace Stevens at least one artist whom professionalism will not demolish." What sort of literary professionalism did you have in mind? And do you find this a feature of America still?

Moore

Yes. I think that writers sometimes lose their verve and their pugnacity, and he never would.

That question I am so often asked: "What work can I find that will enable me to spend my whole time writing?" Charles Ives, the composer, says, "You cannot set art off in a corner and hope for it to have vitality, reality and substance. The fabric weaves itself whole. My work in music helped my business and my work in business helped my music." I am like Charles Ives. Lawrence Durrell and Henry Miller would not agree with me.

Interviewer

But how does professionalism make a writer lose his nerve and pugnacity?

Moore

I suppose money has something to do with it and being regarded as a pundit. Wallace Stevens was really very much annoyed at being catalogued, categorized, and compelled to be scientific about what he was doing—to give satisfaction, to answer the teachers. He wouldn't do that. He was independent.

I think the same of William Carlos Williams. I think he wouldn't make so much of the great American language if he were judicious about everything. And that is the beauty of it—he is willing to be reckless, and if you can't be that, what's the point of the whole thing?

Marianne Moore and Mina Loy

by Ezra Pound

In the verse of Marianne Moore I detect traces of emotion; in that of Mina Loy I detect no emotion whatever. Both of these women are, possibly in unconsciousness, among the followers of Jules Laforgue (whose work shows a great deal of emotion). It is possible, as I have written, or intended to write elsewhere, to divide poetry into three sorts; (1.) melopoeia, to wit, poetry which moves by its music, whether it be a music in the words or an aptitude for, or suggestion of, accompanying music; (2.) imagism, or poetry wherein the feelings of painting and sculpture are predominant (certain men move in phantasmagoria; the images of their gods, whole countrysides, stretches of hill land and forest, travel with them); and there is, thirdly, logopoeia or poetry that is akin to nothing but language, which is a dance of the intelligence among words and ideas and modification of ideas and characters. Pope and the eighteenth-century writers had in this medium a certain limited range. The intelligence of Laforgue ran through the whole gamut of his time. T. S. Eliot has gone on with it. Browning wrote a condensed form of drama, full of things of the senses, scarcely ever pure logopoeia.

One wonders what the devil anyone will make of this sort of thing who has not in his wit all the clues. It has none of the stupidity beloved of the "lyric" enthusiast and the writer and reader who take refuge in scenery description of nature, because they are unable to cope with the human. These two contributors to the "Others" Anthology write logopoeia. It is, in their case, the utterance of clever people in despair, or hovering upon the brink of that precipice. It is of those who have acceded with Renan *"La bêtise humaine est la seule chose qui donne une idée de l'infini."* It is a mind cry, more than a heart cry. "Take the world if thou wilt but leave me an asylum for my affection" is not their lamentation, but rather "In the midst of this desolation, give me at least one intelligence to converse with."

The arid clarity, not without its own beauty, of *le tempérament de l'Americaine,* is in the poems of these two writers. . . .

"Marianne Moore and Mina Loy." From Ezra Pound, "A List of Books," *Little Review,* X (March, 1918), 57–58. Copyright 1918 by Margaret Anderson. Reprinted by permission of Dorothy Pound and New Directions Publishing Corporation.

The point of my praise, for I intend this as praise, even if I do not burst into the phrases of Victor Hugo, is that without any pretences and without clamors about nationality, these girls have written a distinctly national product, they have written something which could not have come out of any other country, and (while I have before now seen a deal of rubbish by both of them) they are interesting and readable (by me, that is).

Marianne Moore (1923)

by T. S. Eliot

Two years ago Miss Moore's book of poems—so far as I know her only book—was published in London by The Egoist Press; and I then undertook to review it for *The Dial*. This promise, for one reason after another, I never fulfilled. Now another poem has appeared, Marriage, published by Manikin, printed apparently in Germany, and with a parenthetical introduction by Mr. Glenway Wescott. Meanwhile I have read Miss Moore's poems a good many times, and always with exactly the same pleasure, and satisfaction in something quite definite and solid. Because of a promise which, because of the long delay, may be considered as having been broken, and because I can only, at the moment, think of five contemporary poets—English, Irish, American, French, and German—whose work excites me as much as, or more than, Miss Moore's, I find myself compelled to say something about them. Not that there is much that is usefully said about any new work of art—I do not rate criticism so highly; but one ought, in honesty, to publish one's beliefs.

Mr. Wescott has, in fact, written a good introduction; I only think that his distinction between proletariat art and aristocratic art is an artificial and unimportant distinction with dangerous consequences. So far as a proletariat art is art at all, it is the same thing in essence as aristocratic art; but in general, and at the present time, the middle-class art, which is what I believe Mr. Wescott to have in mind when he speaks of proletariat art (the proletariat *is* middle class in America) is much more artificial than anything else; it plays with sham ideas, sham emotions, and even sham sensations. On the other hand a real aristocracy is essentially of the same blood as the people over whom it rules: a real aristocracy is not a Baltenland aristocracy of foreign race. This apparently purely political definition applies to art as well: fine art is the *refinement*, not the antithesis, of popular art. Miss Moore's poetry may not seem to confirm this statement. I agree with Mr. Wescott that it is "aristocratic," in that it can only please a very small number of people. But it is not, or not wholly, aristocratic in

"Marianne Moore (1923)." T. S. Eliot's review of *Poems* and *Marriage* by Marianne Moore. From *Dial*, LXXV (December, 1923), 594–97. Copyright 1923 by T. S. Eliot. Reprinted by permission of Mrs. Valerie Eliot.

the Baltenland sense. I see in it at least three elements: a quite new rhythm, which I think is the most valuable thing; a peculiar and brilliant and rather satirical use of what is not, as material, an "aristocratic" language at all, but simply the curious jargon produced in America by universal university education—that jargon which makes it impossible for Americans to talk for half an hour without using the terms of psychoanalysis, and which has introduced "moron" as more forcible than "idiot"; and finally an almost primitive simplicity of phrase. There may be more. Up to the present time Miss Moore has concerned herself with practising and perfecting a given formation of elements; it will depend, I think, on her ability to *shatter* this formation and painfully reconstruct, whether Miss Moore makes another invention equal in merit to the first.

Rhythm, of course, is a highly personal matter; it is not a verse-form. It is always the real pattern in the carpet, the scheme of organization of thought, feeling, and vocabulary, the way in which everything comes together. It is very uncommon. What is certain is that Miss Moore's poems always read very well aloud. That quality is something which no system of scansion can define. It is not separable from the use of words, in Miss Moore's case the conscious and complete appreciation of every word, and in relation to every other word, as it goes by. I think that Those Various Scalpels is an excellent example for study. Here the rhythm depends partly upon the transformation-changes from one image to another, so that the second image is superposed before the first has quite faded, and upon the dexterity of change of vocabulary from one image to another. "Snow sown by tearing winds on the cordage of disabled ships:" has that Latin, epigrammatic succinctness, laconic austerity, which leaps out unexpectedly (altogether in Talisman).

> your raised hand
> an ambiguous signature:

is a distinct shift of manner; it is not an image, but the indication of a fulness of meaning which is unnecessary to pursue.

> blood on the stone floors of French châteaux, with
> regard to which guides are so affirmative:

is a satirical (consciously or unconsciously it does not matter) refinement of that pleasantry (not flippancy, which is something with a more definite purpose) of speech which characterizes the American language, that pleasantry, uneasy, solemn, or self-conscious, which inspires both the jargon of the laboratory and the slang of the comic strip. Miss Moore works this uneasy language of stereotypes—as of a whole people playing uncomfortably at clenches and clevelandisms—with impeccable skill into her pattern. She uses words like "fractional,"

"vertical," "infinitesimal," "astringently"; phrases like "excessive popularity," "a liability rather than an asset," "mask of profundity,"
"vestibule of experience," "diminished vitality," "arrested prosperity."
If this were all, Miss Moore would be no different from her imitators.
The merit consists in the combination, in the other point of view
which Miss Moore possesses at the same time. What her imitators
cannot get are the swift dissolving images, like the mussel shell.

> opening and shutting itself like
> an
> injured fan

and phrases like

> the sea when it proffers flattery in exchange for hemp
> rye, flax, horses, platinum, timber and fur.

> Truth is no Apollo
> Belvedere, no formal thing. The wave may go over it if it likes.

or a magnificence of phrase like

> I recall their magnificence, now not more magnificent
> than it is dim

(how like Valery's *"entre les pins palpite, entre les tombes"* or like his
"eternellement, Eternellement le bout mordre.")

And also they cannot imitate her animals and birds—

> the parrakeet—
> . . . destroying
> bark and portions of the food it could not eat.

  Mr. Wescott, if he agrees with all or even with a part of what I
have written, will probably consider it as an affirmation of his belief
in a kind of "aristocratic" art drawing no sustenance from the soil.
"An aristocratic art, emulating the condition of ritual." But of course
all art emulates the condition of ritual. That is what it comes from
and to that it must always return for nourishment. And nothing
belongs more properly to the people than ritual—or indeed than
aristocracy itself, a popular invention to serve popular needs. (I
suppose the Ku Klux Klan is a popular ritual—as popular as a ritual
can be in a country where there are only variations *within* the middle
class.) Miss Moore's relation to the soil is not a simple one, or rather
it is to various soils—to that of Latium and to that of Attica I
believe (or at least to that of the Aegean littoral) as well as most
positively to the soil (well top-dressed) of America. There are several
reasons (buried in this essay) why Miss Moore's poetry is almost com-

pletely neglected in England, beside the simple reason that it is too good, "in this age of hard striving," to be appreciated anywhere.

And there is one final, and "magnificent" compliment: Miss Moore's poetry is as "feminine" as Christina Rossetti's, one never forgets that it is written by a woman; but with both one never thinks of this particularly as anything but a positive virtue.

Marianne Moore (1925)

by William Carlos Williams

The best work is always neglected and there is no critic among the older men who has cared to champion the newer names from outside the battle. The established critic will not read. So it is that the present writers must turn interpreters of their own work. Even those who enjoy modern work are not always intelligent, but often seem at a loss to know the white marks from the black. But modernism is distressing to many who would at least, due to the necessary appearance of disorder in all immediacy, be led to appreciation through critical study.

If one come with Miss Moore's work to some wary friend and say, "Everything is worthless but the best and this is the best," adding, "only with difficulty discerned" will he see anything, if he be at all well read, but destruction? From my experience he will be shocked and bewildered. He will perceive absolutely nothing except that his whole preconceived scheme of values has been ruined. And this is exactly what he should see, a break through all preconception of poetic form and mood and pace, a flaw, a crack in the bowl. It is this that one means when he says destruction and creation are simultaneous. But this is not easy to accept. Miss Moore, using the same material as all others before her, comes at it so effectively at a new angle as to throw out of fashion the classical conventional poetry to which one is used and puts her own and that about her in its place. The old stops are discarded. This must antagonize many. Furthermore, there is a multiplication, a quickening, a burrowing through, a blasting aside, a dynamization, a flight over—it is modern, but the critic must show that this is only to reveal an essential poetry through the mass, as always, and with superlative effect in this case.

A course in mathematics would not be wasted on a poet, or a reader of poetry, if he remember no more from it than the geometric principle of the intersection of loci: from all angles lines converging and crossing establish points. He might carry it further and say in his imagination that apprehension perforates at places, through to understanding—as white is at the intersection of blue and green and yellow and red. It is this white light that is the background of all good work. Aware of this, one may read the Greeks or the Elizabethans or Sidney Lanier even Robert Bridges, and preserve interest, poise and enjoyment. He may visit Virginia or China, and when friends, eager to please, playfully lead him about for pockets of local color—he may go. Local color is not, as the parodists, the localists believe, an object of art. It is merely a variant serving to locate [an] acme point of white penetration. The intensification of desire toward this purity is the modern variant. It is that which interests me most and seems most solid among the qualities I witness in my contemporaries; it is a quality present in much or even all that Miss Moore does.

Poems, like painting, can be interesting because of the subject with which they deal. The baby glove of a Pharaoh can be so presented as to bring tears to the eyes. And it need not be bad work because it has to do with a favorite cat dead. Poetry, rare and never willingly recognized, only its accidental colors make it tolerable to most. If it be of a red coloration, those who like red will follow and be led restfully astray. So it is with hymns, battle songs, love ditties, elegies. Humanity sees itself in them, it is familiar, the good placed attractively and the bad thrown into a counter light. This is inevitable. But in any anthology it will be found that men have been hard put to it at all times to tell which is poetry and which the impost. This is hard. The difficult thing to realize is that the thrust must go through to the white, at least somewhere.

Good modern work, far from being the fragmentary, neurotic thing its disunderstanders think it, is nothing more than work compelled by these conditions. It is a multiplication of impulses that by their several flights, crossing at all eccentric angles, might enlighten. As a phase, in its slightest beginning, it is more a disc pierced here and there by light; it is really distressingly broken up. But so does any attack seem at the moment of engagement, multiple units crazy except when viewed as a whole.

Surely there is no poetry so active as that of today, so unbound, so dangerous to the mass of mediocrity, if one should understand it, so fleet, hard to capture, so delightful to pursue. It is clarifying in its movements as a wild animal whose walk corrects that of men. Who shall separate the good Whitman from the bad, the dreadful New England maunderers from the others, put air under and around the living and leave the dead to fall dead? Who? None but poems, such as Miss Moore's, their cleanliness, lack of cement, clarity, gentleness. It grows impossible for the eye to rest long upon the object of the drawing. Here is an escape from the old dilemma. The unessential is put rapidly aside as the eye searches between for illumination. Miss Moore undertakes in her work to separate the poetry from the subject entirely—like all the moderns. In this she has been rarely successful and this is important.

Unlike the painters the poet has not resorted to distortions or the abstract in form. Miss Moore accomplishes a like result by rapidity of movement. A poem such as "Marriage" is an anthology of transit. It is a pleasure that can be held firm only by moving rapidly from one thing to the next. It gives the impression of a passage through. There is a distaste for lingering, as in Emily Dickinson. As in Emily Dickinson there is too a fastidious precision of thought where unrhymes fill the purpose better than rhymes. There is a swiftness impaling beauty, but no impatience as in so much present-day trouble with verse. It is a rapidity too swift for touch, a seraphic quality, one might have said yesterday. There is, however, no breast that warms the bars of heaven: it is at most a swiftness that passes without repugnance from thing to thing.

The only help I ever got from Miss Moore toward the understanding of her verse was that she despised connectives. Any other assistance would have been an impoliteness, since she has always been sure of herself if not of others. The complete poem is there waiting: all the wit, the color, the constructive ability (not a particularly strong point that, however). And the quality of satisfaction gathered from reading her is that one may seek long in those exciting mazes sure of coming out at the right door in the end. There is nothing missing but the connectives.

The thought is compact, accurate and accurately planted. In fact, the garden, since it is a garden more than a statue, is found to be curiously of porcelain. It is the mythical, indestructible garden of pleasure, perhaps greatly pressed for space today, but there and intact, nevertheless.

I don't know where, except in modern poetry, this quality of the brittle, highly set-off porcelain garden exists and nowhere in modern work better than Miss Moore. It is this chief beauty of today, this hard crest to nature, that makes the best present work with its "unnatural" appearance seem so thoroughly gratuitous, so difficult to explain, and so doubly a treasure of seclusion. It is the white of a clarity beyond the facts.

There is in the newer work a perfectly definite handling of the materials with a given intention to relate them in a certain way—a handling that is intensely, intentionally selective. There is a definite place where the matters of the day may meet if they choose or not, but if they assemble it must be there. There is no compromise. Miss Moore never falls from the place inhabited by poems. It is hard to give an illustration of this from her work because it is everywhere. One must be careful, though, not to understand this as a mystical support, a danger we are skirting safely, I hope, in our time.

Poe in his most-read first essay quotes Nathaniel Willis' poem "The Two Women," admiringly and in full, and one senses at once the reason: there is a quality to the feeling there that affected Poe tremendously. This mystical quality that endeared Poe to Father Tabb, the poet-priest, still seems to many the essence of poetry itself. It would be idle to name many who have been happily mystical and remained good poets: Poe, Blake, Francis Thompson, et cetera.

But what I wish to point is that there need be no stilled and archaic heaven, no ducking under religiosities to have poetry and to have it stand in its place beyond "nature." Poems have a separate existence uncompelled by nature or the supernatural. There is a "special" place which poems, as all works of art, must occupy, but it it quite definitely the same as that where bricks or colored threads are handled.

In painting, Ingres realized the essentiality of drawing and each perfect part seemed to float free from his work, by itself. There is much in this that applies beautifully to Miss Moore. It is perfect drawing that attains to a separate existence which might, if it please, be called mystical, but is in fact no more than the practicability of design.

To Miss Moore an apple remains an apple whether it be in Eden or the fruit bowl where it curls. But that would be hard to prove—

dazzled by the apple.

The apple is left there, suspended. One is not made to feel that as an apple it has anything particularly to do with poetry or that as such it needs special treatment; one goes on. Because of this, the direct object does seem unaffected. It seems as free from the smears of mystery, as pliant, as "natural" as Venus on the wave. Because of this, her work is never indecorous as where nature is itself concerned. These are great virtues.

Without effort Miss Moore encounters the affairs which concern her as one would naturally in reading or upon a walk outdoors. She is not a Swinburne stumbling to music, but one always finds her moving forward ably, in thought, unimpeded by a rhythm. Her own rhythm is particularly revealing. It does not interfere with her progress; it is the movement of the animal, it does not put itself first and ask the other to follow.

Nor is "thought" the thing that she contends with. Miss Moore uses the thought most interestingly and wonderfully to my mind. I don't know but that this technical excellence is one of the greatest pleasures I get from her. She occupies the thought to its end, and goes on—without connectives. To me this is thrilling. The essence is not broken, nothing is injured. It is a kind hand to a merciless mind at home in the thought as in the cruder image. In the best modern verse, room has been made for the best of modern thought and Miss Moore thinks straight.

Only the most modern work has attempted to do without *ex machina* props of all sorts, without rhyme, assonance, the feudal master beat, the excuse of "nature," of the spirit, mysticism, religiosity, "love," "humor," "death." Work such as Miss Moore's holds its bloom today not by using slang, not by its moral abandon or puritanical stead-fastness, but by the aesthetic pleasure engendered where pure crafts-manship joins hard surfaces skilfully.

Poetry has taken many disguises which by cross reading or intense penetration it is possible to go through to the core. Through inter-section of loci their multiplicity may become revelatory. The sig-nificance of much reading being that this "thing" grow clearer, remain fresh, be more present to the mind. To read more thoroughly than this is idleness; a common classroom absurdity.

One may agree tentatively with Glenway Wescott, that there is a division taking place in America between a proletarian art, full of sincerities, on the one side and an aristocratic and ritualistic art on the other. One may agree, but it is necessary to scrutinize such a statement carefully.

There cannot be two arts of poetry really. There is weight and there is disencumberedness. There can be no schism, except that which has always existed between art and its approaches. There cannot be a proletarian art—even among savages. There is a proletarian taste. To have achieved an organization even of that is to have escaped it.[1]

And to organize into pattern is also, true enough, to "approach the conditions of a ritual." But here I would again go slow. I see only escape from the conditions of ritual in Miss Moore's work: a rush through wind if not toward some patent "end" at least away from pursuit, a pursuit perhaps by ritual. If from such a flight a ritual results it is more the care of those who follow than of the one who leads. "Ritual," too often to suit my ear, connotes a stereo-typed mode of procedure from which pleasure has passed, whereas the poetry to which my attention clings, if it ever knew those condi-tions, is distinguished only as it leaves them behind.

It is at least amusing, in this connection, to quote from *Others,* Volume I, Number 5, November 1915—quoted in turn from J. B. Kerfoot in *Life:* "Perhaps you are unfamiliar with this 'new poetry' that is called 'revolutionary.' It is the expression of democracy of feeling rebelling against an aristocracy of form."

> As if a death mask ever could replace
> Life's faulty excellence!

[1] [Compare T. S. Eliot's discussion of this point in his "Marianne Moore (1923) above, pp. 48–51.]

There are two elements essential to Miss Moore's scheme of composition, the hard and unaffected concept of the apple itself as an idea, then its edge-to-edge contact with the things which surround it— the coil of a snake, leaves at various depths, or as it may be; and without connectives unless it be poetry, the inevitable connective, if you will.

Marriage, through which thought does not penetrate, appeared to Miss Moore a legitimate object for art, an art that would not halt from using thought about it, however, as it might want to. Against marriage, "this institution, perhaps one should say enterprise"— Miss Moore launched her thought not to have it appear arsenaled as in a textbook on psychology, but to stay among apples and giraffes in a poem. The interstices for the light and not the interstitial web of the thought concerned her, or so it seems to me. Thus the material is as the handling: the thought, the word, the rhythm—all in the style. The effect is in the penetration of the light itself, how much, how little; the appearance of the luminous background.

Of marriage there is no solution in the poem and no attempt to make marriage beautiful or otherwise by "poetic" treatment. There is beauty and it is thoughtless, as marriage or a cave inhabited by the sounds and colors of waves, as in the time of prismatic color, as England with its baby rivers, as G. B. Shaw, or chanticleer, or a fish, or an elephant with its strictly practical appendages. All these things are inescapably caught in the beauty of Miss Moore's passage through them; they all have at least edges. This too is a quality that greatly pleases me: definite objects which give a clear contour to her force. Is it a flight, a symphony, a ghost, a mathematic? The usual evasion is to call them poems.

Miss Moore gets great pleasure from wiping soiled words or cutting them clean out, removing the aureoles that have been pasted about them or taking them bodily from greasy contexts. For the compositions which Miss Moore intends, each word should first stand crystal clear with no attachments; not even an aroma. As a cross light upon this, Miss Moore's personal dislike for flowers that have both a satisfying appearance and an odor of perfume is worth noticing. With Miss Moore a word is a word most when it is separated out by science, treated with acid to remove the smudges, washed, dried and placed right side up on a clean surface. Now one may say that this is a word. Now it may be used, and how?

It may be used to smear it again with thinking (the attachments of thought) but in such a way that it will remain scrupulously itself, clean perfect, unnicked beside other words in parade. There must be edges. This casts some light I think on the simplicity of design in much of Miss Moore's work. There must be recognizable edges against the ground which cannot, as she might desire it, be left

entirely white. Prose would be all black, a complete black painted
or etched over, but solid.

There is almost no overlaying at all. The effect is of every object
sufficiently uncovered to be easily recognizable. This simplicity, with
the light coming through from between the perfectly plain masses,
is however extremely bewildering to one who has been accustomed
to look upon the usual "poem," the commonplace opaque board
covered with vain curlicues. They forget, those who would read Miss
Moore aright, that white circular discs grouped closely edge to edge
upon a dark table make black six-pointed stars.

The "useful result" is an accuracy to which this simplicity of
design greatly adds. The effect is for the effect to remain "true";
nothing loses its identity because of the composition, but the parts
in their assembly remain quite as "natural" as before they were gathered. There is no "sentiment"; the softening effect of word upon
word is nil; everything is in the style. To make this ten times evident
is Miss Moore's constant care. There seems to be almost too great
a wish to be transparent and it is here if anywhere that Miss Moore's
later work will show a change, I think.

The general effect is of a rise through the humanities, the sciences,
without evading "thought," through anything (if not everything) of
the best of modern life; taking whatever there is as it comes, using
it and leaving it drained of its pleasure, but otherwise undamaged,
Miss Moore does not compromise science with poetry. In this again,
she is ably modern.

And from this clarity, this acid cleaning, this unblinking will-
ingness, her poems result, a true modern crystallization, the fine essence of today which I have spoken of as the porcelain garden.

Or one will think a little of primitive masonry, the units unglued
and as in the greatest early constructions unstandardized.

In such work as *Critics and Connoisseurs,* and *Poetry,* Miss Moore
succeeds in having the "thing" which is her concern move freely,
unencumbered by the images or the difficulties of thought. In such
work there is no "suggestiveness," no tiresome "subtlety" of trend to
be heavily followed, no painstaking refinement of sentiment. There
is surely a choice evident in all her work, a very definite quality of
choice in her material, a thinness perhaps, but a very welcome and
no little surprising absence of moral tone. The choice being entirely
natural and completely arbitrary is not in the least offensive, in fact it
has been turned curiously to advantage throughout.

From what I have read it was in *Critics and Connoisseurs* that the
successful method used later began first to appear: If a thought presents itself the force moves through it easily and completely: so the
thought also has revealed the "thing"—that is all. The thought is
used exactly as the apple, it is the same insoluble block. In Miss

Moore's work the purely stated idea has an edge exactly like a fruit or a tree or a serpent.

To use anything: rhyme, thought, color, apple, verb—so as to illumine it, is the modern prerogative; a stintless inclusion. It is Miss Moore's success.

The diction, the phrase construction, is unaffected. To use a "poetic" inversion of language, or even such a special posture of speech, still discernible in Miss Moore's earlier work, is to confess an inability to have penetrated with poetry some crevice of understanding; that special things and special places are reserved for art, that it is unable, that it requires fostering. This is unbearable.

Poetry is not limited in that way. It need not say either

> Bound without
> Boundless within.

It has as little to do with the soul as with ermine robes or graveyards. It is not noble, sad, funny. It is poetry. It is free. It is escapeless. It goes where it will. It is in danger, escapes if it can.

This is new! The quality is not new, but the freedom is new, the unbridled leap.

The dangers are thereby multiplied—but the clarity increased. Nothing but the perfect and the clear.

Introduction to *Selected Poems*

by T. S. *Eliot*

We know very little about the value of the work of our contemporaries, almost as little as we know about our own. It may have merits which exist only for contemporary sensibility; it may have concealed virtues which will only become apparent with time. How it will rank when we are all dead authors ourselves we cannot say with any precision. If one is to talk about one's contemporaries at all, therefore, it is important to make up our minds as to what we can affirm with confidence, and as to what must be a matter of doubting conjecture. The last thing, certainly, that we are likely to know about them is their "greatness," or their relative distinction or triviality in relation to the standard of "greatness." For in greatness are involved moral and social relations, relations which can only be perceived from a remoter perspective, and which may be said even to be created in the process of history: we cannot tell, in advance, what any poetry is going to do, how it will operate upon later generations. But the *genuineness* of poetry is something which we have some warrant for believing that a small number, but only a small number, of contemporary readers can recognise. I say positively only a small number, because it seems probable that when any poet conquers a really large public in his lifetime, an increasing proportion of his admirers will admire him for extraneous reasons. Not necessarily for bad reasons, but because he becomes known merely as a symbol, in giving a kind of stimulation, or consolation, to his readers, which is a function of his peculiar relation to them in time. Such effect upon contemporary readers may be a legitimate and proper result of some great poetry, but it has been also the result of much ephemeral poetry.

It does not seem to matter much whether one has to struggle with an age which is unconscious and self-satisfied, and therefore hostile to new forms of poetry, or with one like the present which is self-conscious and distrustful of itself, and avid for new forms which will give it status and self-respect. For many modern readers any superficial novelty of form is evidence of, or is as good as, newness of sensibility;

"Introduction to *Selected Poems*." T. S. Eliot's preface to *Selected Poems* by Marianne Moore (New York: Macmillan Company, 1935; London: Faber & Faber, Ltd., 1935). Copyright 1935 by T. S. Eliot. Reprinted by permission of Mrs. Valerie Eliot.

and if the sensibility is fundamentally dull and second-hand, so much the better; for there is no quicker way of catching an immediate, if transient, popularity, than to serve stale goods in new packages. One of the tests—though it be only a negative test—of anything really new and genuine, seems to be its capacity for exciting aversion among "lovers of poetry."

I am aware that prejudice makes me underrate certain authors: I see them rather as public enemies than as subjects for criticism; and I dare say that a different prejudice makes me uncritically favourable to others. I may even admire the right authors for the wrong reasons. But I am much more confident of my appreciation of the authors whom I admire, than of my depreciation of the authors who leave me cold or who exasperate me. And in asserting that what I call *genuineness* is a more important thing to recognise in a contemporary than *greatness,* I am distinguishing between his function while living and his function when dead. Living, the poet is carrying on that struggle for the maintenance of a living language, for the maintenance of its strength, its subtlety, for the preservation of quality of feeling, which must be kept up in every generation; dead, he provides standards for those who take up the struggle after him. Miss Moore is, I believe, one of those few who have done the language some service in my lifetime.

So far back as my memory extends, which is to the pages of *The Egoist* during the War, and of *The Little Review* and *The Dial* in the years immediately following, Miss Moore has no immediate poetic derivations. I cannot, therefore, fill up my pages with the usual account of influences and development. There is one early poem, *A Talisman,* not reprinted in the text of this volume, which I will quote in full here, because it suggests a slight influence of H. D., certainly of H. D. rather than of any other 'Imagist':

> Under a splintered mast
> Torn from the ship and cast
>   Near her hull,
>
> A stumbling shepherd found
> Embedded in the ground,
>   A sea-gull
>
> Of lapis-lazuli,
> A scarab of the sea,
>   With wings spread—
>
> Curling its coral feet,
> Parting its beak to greet
>   Men long dead.

The sentiment is commonplace, and I cannot see what a bird carved of *lapis-lazuli* should be doing with *coral* feet; but even here the cadence, the use of rhyme, and a certain authoritativeness of manner distinguish the poem. Looking at Miss Moore's poems of a slightly later period, I should say that she had taken to heart the repeated reminder of Mr. Pound: that poetry should be as well written as prose. She seems to have saturated her mind in the perfections of prose, in its precision rather than its purple; and to have found her rhythm, her poetry, her appreciation of the individual word, for herself.

The first aspect in which Miss Moore's poetry is likely to strike the reader is that of minute detail rather than that of emotional unity. The gift for detailed observation, for finding the exact words for some experience of the eye, is liable to disperse the attention of the relaxed reader. The minutiae may even irritate the unwary, or arouse in them only the pleasurable astonishment evoked by the carved ivory ball with eleven other balls inside it, the full-rigged ship in a bottle, the skeleton of the crucifix-fish. The bewilderment consequent upon trying to follow so alert an eye, so quick a process of association, may produce the effect of some "metaphysical" poetry. To the moderately intellectual the poems may appear to be intellectual exercises; only to those whose intellection moves more easily will they immediately appear to have emotional value. But the detail has always its service to perform to the whole. The similes are there for use; as the mussel-shell "opening and shutting itself like an injured fan" (where *injured* has an ambiguity good enough for Mr. Empson), the waves "as formal as the scales on a fish." They make us see the object more clearly, though we may not understand immediately why our attention has been called to this object, and though we may not immediately grasp its association with a number of other objects. So, in her amused and affectionate attention to animals—from the domestic cat, or "to popularize the mule," to the most exotic strangers from the tropics, she succeeds at once in startling us into an unusual awareness of visual patterns, with something like the fascination of a high-powered microscope.

Miss Moore's poetry, or most of it, might be classified as "descriptive" rather than "lyrical" or "dramatic." Descriptive poetry is supposed to be dated to a period, and to be condemned thereby; but it is really one of the permanent modes of expression. In the eighteenth century—or say a period which includes "Cooper's Hill," "Windsor Forest," and Gray's "Elegy"—the scene described is a point of departure for meditations on one thing or another. The poetry of the Romantic Age, from Byron at his worst to Wordsworth at his best, wavers between the reflective and the evocative; but the description, the picture set before you, is always there for the same purpose. The aim of "imagism," so far as I understand it, or so far as it had any, was to induce a peculiar concentration upon something visual, and to set in motion an expanding succession of concentric feelings. Some of Miss Moore's poems—for instance with animal or bird subjects —have a very wide spread of association. It would be difficult to say what is the "subject-matter" of "The Jerboa." For a mind of such agility, and for a sensibility so reticent, the minor subject, such as a pleasant little sand-coloured skipping animal, may be the best release for the major emotions. Only the pedantic literalist could consider the subject-matter to be trivial; the triviality is in himself. We all have to choose whatever subject-matter allows us the most powerful and most secret release; and that is a personal affair.

The result is often something that the majority will call frigid; for feeling in one's own way, however intensely, is likely to look like frigidity to those who can only feel in accepted ways.

> The deepest feeling always shows itself in silence;
> not in silence, but restraint.

It shows itself in a control which makes possible the fusion of the ironic-conversational and the high-rhetorical, as

> I recall their magnificence, now not more magnificent
> than it is dim. It is difficult to recall the ornament,
>   speech, and precise manner of what one might
>   call the minor acquaintances twenty
>   years back. . . .
>   strict with tension, malignant
> in its power over us and deeper
>   than the sea when it proffers flattery in exchange
>   for hemp,
>   rye, flax, horses, platinum, timber and fur.

As one would expect from the kind of activity which I have been trying to indicate, Miss Moore's versification is anything but "free." Many of the poems are in exact, and sometimes complicated, formal patterns, and move with the elegance of a minuet. ("Elegance," indeed, is one of her certain attributes.) Some of the poems (e.g. "Marriage," "An Octopus") are unrhymed; in others (e.g. "Sea Unicorns and Land Unicorns") rhyme or assonance is introduced irregularly, in a number of the poems rhyme is part of a regular pattern interwoven with unrhymed endings. Miss Moore's use of rhyme is in itself a definite innovation in metric.

In the conventional forms of rhyme the stress given by the rhyme tends to fall in the same place as the stress given by the sense. The extreme case, at its best, is the pentameter couplet of Pope. Poets before and after Pope have given variety, sometimes at the expense of smoothness, by deliberately separating the stresses, from time to time; but this separation—often effected simply by longer periods or more involved syntax—can hardly be considered as more than a deviation from the norm for the purpose of avoiding monotony. The tendency of some of the best contemporary poetry is of course to dispense with rhyme altogether; but some of those who do use it have used it here and there to make a pattern directly in contrast with the sense and rhythm pattern, to give a greater intricacy. Some of the internal rhyming of Hopkins is to the point. (Genuine or auditory internal rhyme must not be confused with false or visual internal rhyme. If a poem reads just as well when cut up so that all the rhymes fall at the end of lines, then the internal rhyme is false and only a typographical caprice, as in Oscar Wilde's "Sphinx.") This rhyme, which forms a pattern *against* the metric and sense pattern of the poem, may be either heavy or light—that is to say, either *heavier* or *lighter* than the other pattern. The two kinds, heavy and light, have doubtless different uses which remain to be explored. Of the *light* rhyme Miss Moore is the greatest living master; and indeed she is the first, so far as I know, who has investigated its possibilities. It will be observed that the effect sometimes requires giving a word a slightly more analytical pronunciation, or stressing a syllable more than ordinarily:

> al-
> ways has been—at the antipodes from the init-
> ial great truths. 'Part of it was crawling, part of it
> was about to crawl, the rest
> was torpid in its lair.' In the short-legged, fit-
> ful advance. . . .

It is sometimes obtained by the use of articles as rhyme words:

> an
> injured fan.
> The barnacles which encrust the side
> of the wave, cannot hide . . .

> the
> turquoise sea
> of bodies. The water drives a wedge . . .

In a good deal of what is sometimes (with an unconscious theological innuendo) called "modernist" verse one finds either an excess or a defect of technical attention. The former appears in an emphasis upon words rather than things, and the latter in an emphasis upon things and an indifference to words. In either case, the poem is formless, just as the most accomplished sonnet, if it is an attempt to express matter unsuitable for sonnet form, is formless. But a precise fitness of form and matter mean also a balance between them: thus the form, the pattern movement, has a solemnity of its own (e.g. Shakespeare's songs), however light and gay the human emotion concerned; and a gaiety of its own, however serious or tragic the emotion. The choruses of Sophocles, as well as the songs of Shakespeare, have another concern besides the human action of which they are spectators, and without this other concern there is not poetry. And on the other hand, if you aim only at the poetry in poetry, there is no poetry either.

My conviction, for what it is worth, has remained unchanged for the last fourteen years: that Miss Moore's poems form part of the small body of durable poetry written in our time; of that small body of writings, among what passes for poetry, in which an original sensibility and alert intelligence and deep feeling have been engaged in maintaining the life of the English language. . . .

The Method of Marianne Moore

by R. P. Blackmur

In making a formal approach to Marianne Moore, that is in de-liberately drawing back and standing aside from the flux and fabric of long reading to see where the flux flowed and how the fabric was made, what at once predominates is the need for special terms and special adjustments to meet the texture and pattern of her poems. So only can the substance be reconciled and brought home to the general body of poetry; so only, that is, can the substance be made available and availing. The facts are clear enough and many of them even obvious to a wakened attention; the problem is to name them with names that both discriminate her work and relate it—if only in parallel—to other work with which it is cognate. Time and wear are the usual agents of this operation, whereby mutual interpenetration is effected between the new and old—always to be re-discriminated for closer contact—and the new becomes formally merely another re-source of the art. Here we may assist and provisionally anticipate a little the processes of time and wear. What we make is a fiction to school the urgency of reading; no more; for actually we must return to the verse itself in its own language and to that felt appreciation of it to which criticism affords only overt clues.

In making up our own fiction let us turn first to some of those with which Miss Moore herself supplies us; which we may do all the more readily and with less wariness because she is so plainly responsi-ble and deliberate in her least use of language—being wary only not to push illustrations past intention, insight, and method, into the dark. Substance is the dark, otherwise to be known.[1] And this is itself

---

"The Method of Marianne Moore." From *The Double Agent, Essays in Craft and Elucidation* by R. P. Blackmur (New York, 1935). Reprinted in *Language as Gesture* by R. P. Blackmur. Copyright 1952 by R. P. Blackmur. Reprinted by per-mission of Harcourt, Brace & World, Inc. and George Allen & Unwin Ltd.

[1] As Matthew Arnold distinguished between descriptions of nature written in "the Greek way" and those written in "the faithful way," and made his distinction fruitful, we might, without being too solemn about it, distinguish between the content of verse taken on a rational, conventional plane, and the content, itself non-rational and unique, which can be reached only *through* the rational form and conventional scaffold.

the nub of the first illustration. I quote complete "The Past is the Present." [2]

> If external action is effete
> and rhyme is outmoded,
> I shall revert to you,
> Habakkuk, as on a recent occasion I was goaded
> into doing by XY, who was speaking of unrhymed verse.
> This man said—I think that I repeat
> his identical words:
> 'Hebrew poetry is
> prose with a sort of heightened consciousness.' Ecstasy affords
> the occasion and expediency determines the form.

It is a delicate matter to say here only the guiding thing, both to avoid expatiation and to point the issue. I wish of course to enforce the last period, very possibly in a sense Miss Moore might not expect, yet in Miss Moore's terms too. A poem, so far as it is well-made for its own purpose, predicts much of which the author was not aware; as a saw cannot be designed for *all* its uses. Nor do the predictions emerge by deviling scripture, but rather by observation of the organic development of the words as they play upon each other. A poem is an idiom and surpasses the sum of its uses. [3]

For ease of approach let us take the last and slightest fact first. In Miss Moore's work inverted commas are made to perform significantly and notably and with a fresh nicety which is part of her contribution to the language. Besides the normal uses to determine quotation or to indicate a special or ironic sense in the material enclosed or as a kind of minor italicization, they are used as boundaries for units of association which cannot be expressed by grammar and syntax. They are used sometimes to impale their contents for close examination, sometimes to take their contents as in a pair of tongs for gingerly or derisive inspection, sometimes to gain the isolation of superiority or vice versa—in short for all the values of setting matter off, whether in eulogy or denigration. As these are none of them arbitrary but are all extensions and refinements of the common uses, the reader will find himself carried along, as by rhyme,

[2] Text of all quotations from *Selected Poems*, with an Introduction by T. S. Eliot, New York, The Macmillan Co., 1935. This differs from the earlier *Observations* (New York, The Dial Press, 1925) by the addition of eight poems and the omission of fourteen. Most of the reprinted poems have been revised slightly, one or two considerably, and one is entirely rewritten and much expanded.

[3] Put the other way round we can borrow, for what it is worth, a mathematician's definition of number and apply it to poetry. A poem is, we can say, like any number, "the class of all classes having the properties of a given class"; it is ready for all its uses, but is itself "only" the class to which the uses belong. The analogue should not be pushed, as its virtue is in its incongruity and as afterthought.

to full appreciation. Which brings us with undue emphasis to the
inverted commas in this poem. In earlier versions the last three lines
were enclosed; here the second sentence, which is crucial to the poem,
stands free, and thus gains a strength of isolation without being any
further from its context, becoming in fact nearer and having a more
direct relation to the *whole* poem: so much so that the earlier pointing must seem to have been an oversight. Once part of what the man
said, part of his identical words, it is now Miss Moore's or the poem's
comment on what the man said and the conclusion of the poem. So
read, we have in this sentence not only a parallel statement to the
statement about Hebrew poetry but also a clue to the earlier lines.
It is what the rest of the poem builds to and explains; and it in its
turn builds back and explains and situates the rest of the poem. And
it is the pointing, or at any rate the comparison of the two pointings,
which makes this clear. If it were a mere exercise of Miss Moore's
and our own in punctuation, then as it depended on nothing it would
have nothing to articulate. But Miss Moore's practice and our appreciation are analogous in scope and importance to the score in
music. By a refinement of this notion Mr. Eliot observes in his Introduction that "many of the poems are in exact, and sometimes complicated formal patterns, and move with the elegance of a minuet." It
is more than that and the very meat of the music, and one need not
tire of repeating it because it *ought* to be obvious. The pattern establishes, situates, and organizes material which without it would have
no life, and as it enlivens it becomes inextricably a part of the material; it participates as well as sets off. The only difficulty in ap-
prehending this lies in our habit of naming only the conventional or
abstract aspects of the elements of the pattern, naming never their
enactment.[4]

So far we exemplify generally that ecstasy affords the occasion and
expediency determines the form. We perceive the occasion and seize
the nearest peg to hang the form on, which happened to be the very
slight peg of inverted commas. Working backward, we come on Hebrew poetry and Habakkuk, one of its more rhetorical practitioners.
Hebrew poetry (not to say the Bible) is used throughout Miss Moore's
work as a background ideal and example of poetic language, an ideal,
however, not directly to be served but rather kept in mind for impetus,
reference, and comparison. A good part of the poem "Novices" is
eulogy of Hebrew poetry. Here, in this poem, we have Habakkuk,
who has a special as well as a representative business. As a poet
Habakkuk was less than the Psalmist or Solomon or Job; nor had he
the pith of the Proverbs or the serenity of Ecclesiastes. His service

---

[4] Whether this is a defect of language or of thinking I leave to I. A. Richards
who alone has the equipment (among critics) and the will to determine.

here is in the fact that he was a prophet of the old school, a praiser of gone times, a man goaded, as Miss Moore is, into crying out against the spiritual insufficience and formal decay of the times. The goading was the occasion of his ecstasy; anathema and prayer his most expedient—his most satisfactory—form. Miss Moore is speaking of matters no less serious; she couples external action and rhyme; and for her the expedient form is a pattern of elegant balances and compact understatement. It is part of the virtue of her attack upon the formless in life and art that the attack should show the courtesy and aloofness of formal grace. There is successful irony, too, in resorting through masterly rhymes to Habakkuk, who had none, and who would no doubt have thought them jingling and effete. (The rhymes have also the practical function of binding the particles of the poem. The notions which compound the poem mutually modify each other, as Coleridge and Mr. Richards would prescribe, and reach an equivalence; and the medium in which the modifications flow or circulate is emphasized and echoed in the rhymes.)

We note above that external action and rhyme are coupled, a juxtaposition which heightens the importance of each. If we conceive Habakkuk presiding upon it the import of the association should become clear. In the first line, "If external action is effete," the word *effete* is a good general pejorative, would have been suitable for Habakkuk in his capacity of goaded prophet. External action is the bodying forth of social life and when we call it effete we say the worst of it. Effete is a word much used of civilizations in decline—Roman, Byzantine, Persian—to represent that kind of sophistication which precedes the relapse into barbarism. What is effete may yet be bloody, stupid, and cruel, and its very refinements are of these. In the effete is the *flowering* of the vicious, a flowering essentially formless because without relation to the underlying substance. Thus, by Habakkuk, we find the morals implicit in the poem. Again, the poem may be taken declaratively (but only if it is tacitly held to include the implicit); if society and literature are in such shape that I cannot follow immediate traditions, well, I shall appeal to something still older. It is all the same. Ecstasy affords the occasion and expediency determines the form, whether I think of life or art.

I have, I think, laid out in terms of a lowered consciousness, a good deal of the material of this poem; but the reader need not think the poem has disappeared or its least fabric been injured. It is untouched. Analysis cannot touch but only translate for preliminary purposes the poem the return to which every sign demands. What we do is simply to set up clues which we can name and handle and exchange whereby we can make available all that territory of the poem which we cannot name or handle but only envisage. We emphasize the technique, as the artist did in fact, in order to come at the substance which the technique employed. Naturally, we do not emphasize all the aspects of the technique since that would involve discussion of more specific problems of language than there are words in the poem, and bring us, too, to all the problems of meaning which are *not* there.[5] We select, rather, those formal aspects which are most readily demonstrable: matters like rhyme and pattern and punctuation, which appear to control because they accompany a great deal else; and from these we reach necessarily, since the two cannot be detached except in the confusion of controversy, into the technical aspects, the conventional or general meanings of the words arranged by the form: as exemplified here by Habakkuk and the word effete. We show, by an analysis which always conveniently stops short, a selection of the ways in which the parts of a poem bear on each other; and we believe, by experience, that we thereby become familiar with what the various tensions produce: the poem itself. This belief is of an arbitrary or miraculous character, and cannot be defended except by customary use. It should perhaps rather be put that as the poet requires his technique (which is not his knowledge) before he can put his poem on paper, so the reader requires a thorough awareness of technique (which again is not *his* knowledge) before he can read the poem. However that may be— and the best we can do is a doubtful scaffold of terms—the point here is that all that can ever actually be brought into the discussion of a poem is its technical aspects. Which happens in all but the best poetry to be very near the whole of it. Here, in Miss Moore's poem, "The Past is the Present," we might provisionally risk the assertion that the last line is the surd of the "poetry" in it. The rest both leads up to it and is suffused by it. The rest is nothing without it; and it would itself remain only a dislocated aphorism, lacking poetry, without the rest. "Ecstasy affords the occasion and expediency determines the form."

  As it happens the line is actually pertinent as a maxim for Miss Moore's uncollected poetics; its dichotomy is at the intellectual base of all her work; and if we examine next the poem called "Poetry" we shall find Miss Moore backing us up in carefully measured understatement neatly placed among expedient ornament. But let us put off examination of the poem as such, and consider first what there is in it that may be translated to intellectual terms. The poem will outlast us and we shall come to it perhaps all the more sensi-

---

[5] A perspective of just such a literally infinite labor is presented in I. A. Richards' *Mencius and the Mind,* which is fascinating but engulfing; as the opposite perspective is presented by the same author (with C. K. Ogden) in various works on Basic English, which combines the discipline of ascetic poverty with the expansiveness of, in a few hundred words, verbal omniscience. But I quote from Miss Moore's "Picking and Choosing," with I hope no more solemnity than the text affords: "We are not daft about the meaning but this familiarity with wrong meanings puzzles one."

tively for having libeled it; and it may indeed luckily turn out that our libel is the subject of the poem: that certainly will be the underlying set of argument. To translate is to cross a gap and the gap is always dark. Well then, whatever the injustice to the poem and to Miss Moore as an esthetician, the following notions may be abstracted from the text for purposes of discourse and amusement. Since these purposes are neither dramatic nor poetic the order in which the notions are here displayed is not that in which they appear in the poem.

Miss Moore's poem says, centrally, that we cannot have poetry—until poets can be "literalists of the imagination." The phrase is made from one in W. B. Yeats's essay, "William Blake and the Imagination." The cogent passage in Yeats reads: "The limitation of his [Blake's] view was from the very intensity of his vision; he was a too literal realist of the imagination, as others are of nature; and because he believed that the figures seen by the mind's eye, when exalted by inspiration, were 'eternal essences,' symbols or divine essences, he hated every grace of style that might obscure their lineaments." Yeats first printed his essay in 1897; had he written it when he wrote his postscript, in 1924, when he, too, had come to hate the graces which obscure, he would, I think, have adopted Miss Moore's shorter and wholly eulogistic phrase and called Blake simply a "literalist of the imagination," [6] and found some other words to explain Blake's excessively arbitrary symbols. At any rate, in Miss Moore's version, the phrase has a bearing on the poem's only other overt reference, which is to Tolstoy's exclusion of "business documents and school books" from the field of poetry. Here her phrase leads to a profound and infinitely spreading distinction. Poets who can present, as she says they must, "imaginary gardens with real toads in them," ought also to be able to present, and indeed will if their interest lies that way, real school books and documents. The whole flux of experience and interpretation is appropriate subject matter to an imagination *literal* enough to see the poetry in it; an imagination, that is, as intent on the dramatic texture (on what is involved, is tacit, is immanent) of the quotidian, as the imagination of the painter is intent, in Velasquez, on the visual texture of lace. One is reminded here, too, of T. S. Eliot's dogma in reverse: "The spirit killeth; the letter giveth life"; and as with Eliot the result of his new trope is to refresh the original form by removing from it the *dead* part of its convention, so Miss Moore's object is to exalt the imagination at the expense of its conventional appearances. Her gardens are imaginary, which makes possible the reality of her toads. Your commonplace

[6] My quotation is taken from the collected edition of Yeats's essays, New York, 1924, page 147; Miss Moore's reference, which I have not checked, was to the original *Ideas of Good and Evil*, printed some twenty years earlier by A. H. Bullen.

mind would have put the matter the other way round—with the
good intention of the same thing—and would have achieved nothing
but the sterile assertion of the imagination as a portmanteau of stereotypes: which is the most part of what we are used to see carried, by
all sorts of porters, as poetic baggage.

It is against them, the porters and their baggage, that Miss Moore
rails when she begins her poem on poetry with the remark: "I, too,
dislike it: there are things that are important beyond all this fiddle."
But in the fiddle, she discovers, there is a place for the genuine.
Among the conventions of expression there is the possibility of
vivid, particularized instances:

> Hands that can grasp, eyes
> that can dilate, hair that can rise
> if it must,

and so on. Such hands, hair, and eyes are, we well know, props and
crises of poetastry, and are commonly given in unusable, abstract
form, mere derivative gestures we can no longer feel; as indeed their
actual experience may also be. They remain, however, exemplars of the
raw material of poetry. If you take them literally and make them
genuine in the garden of imagination, then, as the poem says, "you are
interested in poetry." You have seen them in ecstasy, which is only to
say beside themselves, torn from their demeaning context; and if you
are able to give them a new form or to refresh them with an old
form—whichever is more expedient—then you will have accomplished
a poem.

Perhaps I stretch Miss Moore's intentions a little beyond the pale;
but the process of her poem itself I do not think I have stretched
at all—have merely, rather, presented one of the many possible descriptions by analogue of the poetic process she actually employs.
The process, like any process of deliberate ecstasy, involves for the
reader as well as the writer the whole complex of wakened sensibility,
which, once awakened, must be both constrained and driven along,
directed and freed, fed and tantalized, sustained by reason to the
very point of seeing, in every rational datum—I quote from another
poem, "Black Earth"—the "beautiful element of unreason under it."
The quotidian, having been shown as genuine, must be shown no less
as containing the strange, as saying more than appears, and, even
more, as containing the print of much that cannot be said at all. Thus
we find Miss Moore constantly presenting images the most explicit but
of a kind containing inexhaustibly the inexplicable—whether in gesture or sentiment. She gives what we know and do not know; she
gives in this poem, for example, "elephants pushing, a wild horse
taking a roll, a tireless wolf under a tree," and also "the baseball

fan, the statistician." We can say that such apposites are full of re-minding, or that they make her poem husky with unexhausted detail, and we are on safe ground; but we have not said the important thing, we have not named the way in which we are illuminated, nor shown any sign at all that we are aware of the major operation performed—in this poem (elsewhere by other agents)—by such ap-positions. They are as they succeed the springboards—as when they fail they are the obliterating quicksands—of ecstasy. In their variety and their contrasts they force upon us two associated notions; first we are led to see the elephant, the horse, the wolf, the baseball fan, and the statistician, as a group or as two groups detached by their given idiosyncrasies from their practical contexts, we see them beside themselves, for themselves alone, like the lace in Velasquez or the water-lights in Monet; and secondly, I think, we come to be aware, whether consciously or not, that these animals and these men are themselves, in their special activities, obsessed, freed, and beside them-selves. There is an exciting quality which the pushing elephant and the baseball fan have in common; and our excitement comes in feel-ing that quality, so integral to the apprehension of life, as it were beside and for itself, not in the elephant and the fan, but in terms of the apposition in the poem.

Such matters are not credibly argued and excess of statement per-haps only confuses import and exaggerates value. As it happens, which is why this poem is chosen rather than another, the reader can measure for himself exactly how valuable this quality is; he can read the "same" poem with the quality dominant and again with the quality hardly in evidence. On page 31 in *Observations* the poem appears in thirteen lines; in *Selected Poems* it has either twenty-nine or thirty, depending on how you count the third stanza. For myself, there is the difference between the poem and no poem at all, since the later version delivers—where the earlier only announces—the letter of imagination. But we may present the differences more con-cretely, by remarking that in the earlier poem half the ornament and all the point are lacking. What is now clearly the dominant emphasis —on poets as literalists of the imagination—which here germinates the poem and gives it career, is not even implied in the earlier version. The poem did not get that far, did not, indeed, become a poem at all. What is now a serious poem on the nature of esthetic reality remained then a half-shrewd, half-pointless conceit against the willfully obscure. But it is not, I think, this rise in level from the innocuous to the penetrating, due to any gain in the strength of Miss Moore's con-ception. The conception, the idea, now that we know what it is, may be as readily inferred in the earlier version as it is inescapably felt in the later, but it had not in the earlier version been articulated and composed, had no posture to speak of, had lacked both development

and material to develop: an immature product. The imaginary garden
was there but there were no real toads in it.

What we have been saying is that the earlier version shows a failure
in the technique of making a thought, the very substantial failure to
know when a thought is complete and when it merely adverts to itself
and is literally insufficient. There is also—as perhaps there must always be in poetry that fails—an accompanying insufficience of verbal
technique, in this instance an insufficience of pattern and music as
compared to the later version. Not knowing, or for the moment not
caring, what she had to do, Miss Moore had no way of choosing and
no reason for using the tools of her trade. Miss Moore is to an extent
a typographic poet, like Cummings or Hopkins; she employs the effects of the appearance and arrangement of printed words as well as
their effects sounding in the ear: her words are in the end far more
printed words than the words of Yeats, for example, can ever be. And
this is made clear by the earlier version which lacks the *printed* effect
rather than by the later version which exhibits it. When we have
learned how, we often do not notice what we appreciate but rather
what is not there to *be* appreciated.

But if we stop and are deliberate, by a stroke cut away our intimacy
with the poem, and regard it all round for its physiognomy, an object
with surfaces and signs, we see immediately that the later version
looks better on the page, has architecture which springs and suggests
deep interiors; we notice the rhymes and the stanza where they are
missing and how they multiply heavily, *both to the ear and the eye,*
in the last stanza; we notice how the phrasing is marked, how it is
shaded, and how, in the nexus of the first and second stanzas, it is
momentarily confused: we notice, in short, not how the poem was
made—an operation intractable to any description—but what about
it, now that it is made, will strike and be felt by the attentive ex-
aminer. Then turning back to the earlier version, knowing that it has
pretty much the same heart, give as much occasion for ecstasy, we see
indefeasibly why it runs unpersuasively through the mind, and why
the later, matured version most persuasively invades us. It is no use
saying that Miss Moore has herself matured—as evidence the notion
is inadmissible; the concept or idea or thought of the poem is not
difficult, new or intense, but its presentation, in the later version, is
all three. She found, as Yeats would say, the image to call out the
whole idea; that was one half. The other half was finding how to
dress out the image to its best advantage, so as to arouse, direct,
sustain, and consolidate attention.

That is not, or hardly at all, a question of Miss Moore's personal
maturity; as may be shown, I think, if we consult two poems, presumably more or less as early as the earlier version of "Poetry." One
is a poem which Miss Moore omits from her *Selected Poems,* but which

Mr. Eliot neatly reprints in his Introduction, called "The Talisman."
In the light of what we have been saying, Miss Moore was right in
omitting it (as she was mainly right in omitting thirteen other poems);
it lacks the fundamental cohesiveness of a thing made complete: with
a great air of implying everything, it implies almost nothing. Yet Mr.
Eliot was right in quoting it, and for the reasons given; it shows a
mastery of heavy rhyme which produces its fatal atmosphere, and it
shows that authoritative manner of speech-English which is one device
to achieve persuasion. But the omission is more justifiable than the
quotation; the substantial immaturity of the poem diseases the maturity of the form and makes it specious, like the brightness of fevered
eyes.

The other poem, "Silence," which I quote, Miss Moore reprints
verbatim except for the addition of a single letter to perfect the
grammar and the omission of double quotes in the next to last line.

> My father used to say,
> 'Superior people never make long visits,
> have to be shown Longfellow's grave
> or the glass flowers at Harvard.
> Self-reliant like the cat—
> that takes its prey to privacy,
> the mouse's limp tail hanging like a shoelace from its mouth—
> they sometimes enjoy solitude,
> and can be robbed of speech
> by speech that has delighted them.
> The deepest feeling always shows itself in silence;
> not in silence, but restraint.'
> Nor was he insincere in saying, 'Make my house your inn.'
> Inns are not residences.

There was no reason for change, only for scruples maintained and
minute scrutiny; for the poem reaches that limit of being—both in
the life of what it is about and in that other, musical life which is
the play of a special joining of words—which we call maturity. It is
important to emphasize here what commonly we observe last, namely
the magnitude or scope of the poem; otherwise the sense of its maturity is lost. The magnitude is small but universal within the universe
of those who distinguish cultivated human relations, which leaves us
all the room we need to grow while reading the poem; and which
signifies, too, that we should only diminish the value and injure the
genuineness of the poem if we held its magnitude greater, its reach
further. Thus the reader must contribute his sense of its maturity to
the poem before it can be situated, before, as Wallace Stevens says,
we can "let be be the finale of seem."

There is here the spirit of an old controversy which we need not

re-enter, but which we ought to recognize in order to pass it by: the
controversy about young men writing great poems and old men going
to seed, about Wordsworth of the Lyrical Ballards and Wordsworth
wordsworthian. It is a popular controversy in various senses of that
adjective. A more pertinent phrasing of the seminal problem, by
which we should escape the false controversy, is, I think, a phrasing
in terms of the question of maturity; and the point is that there are
various orders of maturity with complex mutually related conditions
required to produce each. There are the broad and obvious classes of
conditions which we list under the heads of technical competence and
underlying import; but we do not, in actual poems, ever have import
without competence or competence without import. Trouble rises
from the confusion of import with intellectually demonstrable content,
and technical competence with *mere* skill of execution. The music of
words alone may lift common sentiment to great import, e.g., Take,
O take those lips away; or at any rate we are faced with much great
poetry which has only commonplace intellectual content and yet af-
fects our fundamental convictions. Again—and I do not mean to leave
the realm of poetry—we have, as an example of halfway house, such
things as the best speeches in *The Way of the World,* where an effect
like that of music and like that of thought, too, is had without full
recourse to either, but rather through the perfection of the spoken
word alone. And at the other end we have the great things in the
great poets that do not *appear* to depend upon anything but their
own barest bones. It is hard here to give an example beyond suspicion.
There is Paolo's speech at the end of *Inferno* V, Blake's Time is the
mercy of eternity, Shakespeare's Ripeness is all, perhaps the Epilogue
to *The Poetaster.* The point is that a balance must be struck of complex conditions so that nothing is too much and nothing not enough;
but most of all it must be remembered that the balance of conditions
which produced maturity in one place will not necessarily produce it
in another. Nor is it just to judge the maturity of one poem by standards brought from another order of poetry; nor, lastly, does the maturity of a poem alone determine its magnitude. Drayton's "The
Parting," the ballad "Waly Waly," and *Antony and Cleopatra,* are all,
and equally, mature poetry. *Hamlet,* we say, has a sick place in it, and
for us the first part of the first act of *King Lear* is puerile; but we do
not judge *Hamlet* and *Lear* in terms of Drayton or the balladist, although we may, for certain purposes, apply to them the special perfection of *Antony.* Maturity is the touchstone of achievement, not of
magnitude.

Returning to Miss Moore's "Silence," let us see if we can what
balance it is she has struck to bring it to a maturity which makes the
question of magnitude for the moment irrelevant. The outer aids and
props familiar in her best verse are either absent or negligible. The

poem has no imposed, repetitive pattern, no rhyme for emphasis or sound, it calls particularly neither upon the eye nor the ear; it ignores everywhere the advantage of referring the reader, for strength, to any but the simplest elements of overt form—the rudiment of continuous iambic syllabification, which prevails in all but one line. Only one phrase—that about the mouse's limp tail—is specifically characteristic of Miss Moore; all the rest of the phrasing represents cultivated contemporary idiom, heightened, as we see at first glance, because set apart.

Here is one of the secrets—perhaps we ought to say one of the dominant fixed tropes—of Miss Moore's verse; and it is here what she has relied upon almost altogether. She resorts, or rises like a fish, continually to the said thing, captures it, sets it apart, points and polishes it to bring out just the special quality she heard in it. Much of her verse has the peculiar, unassignable, indestructible authority of speech overheard—which often means so much precisely because we do not know what was its limiting, and dulling, context. The quality in her verse that carries over the infinite possibilities of the overheard, is the source and agent of much of her power to give a sense of invading reality; and it does a good deal to explain what Mr. Eliot, in his Introduction, calls her authoritativeness of manner—which is a different thing from a sense of reality.

It does not matter that Miss Moore frequently works the other way round, abstracting her phrase from a guidebook, an advertisement, or a biography; what matters is that whatever her sources she treats her material as if it were quoted, isolated speech, and uses it, not as it was written or said—which cannot be known—but for the purpose which, taken beside itself, seems in it paramount and most appropriate. In "Silence" she takes phrases from Miss A. M. Homans and from Prior's life of Edmund Burke, and combines them in such a way that they declare themselves more fully, because isolated, emphasized, and lit by the incongruous image of the cat and the mouse, than either could have declared themselves in first context. The poet's labor in this respect is similar to that of a critical translation where, by selection, exclusion, and rearrangement a sense is emphasized which was found only on a lower level and diffusely in the original; only here there is no damage by infidelity but rather the reward of deep fidelity to what, as it turns out, was really there waiting for emphasis.

But besides the effect of heightened speech, Miss Moore relies also and as deeply upon the rhetorical device of understatement—by which she gains, as so many have before her, a compression of substance which amounts to the fact of form. Form is, after all, the way things are put, and it may be profitably though not finally argued that every device of saying is an element in the form of what is said, whether it

be detachable and predictable like the stress of a syllable or inextrica-
ble and innate like the tone of a thought. Understatement is a mis-
nomer in every successful instance, as it achieves exactly what it pretends not to do: the fullest possible order of statement consonant with
the mode of language employed. In such classic examples as Shakespeare's "The rest is silence," or Wordsworth's "But oh, the difference to me!" who shall suggest that more could have been said another way? who rather will not believe that it is in phrases such as
these that the radical failure of language (its inability ever explicitly
to *say* what is in a full heart) is overcome? Never, surely, was there a
poorer name for such a feat of imagination: what we call understatement is only secured when we have charged ordinary words with
extraordinary content, content not naturally in words at all. But they
must be the right words nonetheless. Did not Shakespeare and Wordsworth really state to the limit matters for which there are no large
words, matters which must, to be apprehended at all, be invested in
common words?

Such is the archetype, the seminal expectation of understatement,
and Miss Moore's poem, on its special plane, subscribes to it. But
we are here concerned more with its subordinate, its ancillary uses
—with its composition with operative irony and with its use to avoid
a *conventional form* while preserving the conventional intention in all
freshness. These are the uses with which we are familiar in daily life—
crassly in sarcasm and finely in shrewd or reasonable wit; and it is on
the plane of daily life and what might be said there—only heightened
and rounded off for inspection—that this poem is written. It is part of
the understatement, in the sense here construed, that superior people
should be compared not to the gods accredited to the great world but
to the cat carrying a mouse into a corner. The advantage is double.
By its very incongruity—its quaintness, if you will—the comparison
forces into prominence the real nature of the following notion of
chosen solitude. We cut away immediately all that does not belong
to the business of the poem; and find ourselves possessed of a new
point of view thrown up and "justified" by the contrast. By a proud
irony, content barely to indicate itself, the conventional views of solitude and intimacy are both destroyed and re-animated. A similar effect is secured in the last two lines—perhaps most emphatically in
the choice of the word *residences,* itself, in this context, an understatement for the emotional word *homes* that detonates far more than
the word *homes* could have done.

Finally, it is perhaps worth noting that "Make my house your
inn" is both an understatement and a different statement of Burke's
intention. Burke did not have the glass flowers, nor cats proud with
mice, preceding his invitation: "Throw yourself into a coach," said
he. "Come down and make my house your inn." But Miss Moore

heard the possibility and set it free with all it implied. That is the poem. As the reader agrees that it is successful without recourse to the traditional overt forms of the art, he ought perhaps to hold that its virtue rises from recourse to the mystery, the fount of implication, in the spoken word combined with a special use of understatement. It makes a sample of the paradigm in its purest order, but hardly its least complex. The ecstasy was of speech, the expediency the greatest economy of means—as it happened in this poem, understatement. Yet as it is genuine, the spirit of its imagination is seen through the letter of what the speech might say.

All this is meant to be accepted as a provisional statement of Miss Moore's practical esthetic—to denominate the ways her poems are made and to suggest the variety of purposes they serve. As it is acceptable, subject to modification and growth in any detail, it should be applicable elsewhere in her work, and if applied make intimacy easier. It may be profitable in that pursuit to examine lightly a selection of the more complex forms—both outward and inward—in which her work is bodied. Miss Moore is a poet bristling with notable facts—especially in the technical quarter—and it would be shameful in an essay at all pretentious not to make some indication of their seductiveness and their variety.

She is an expert in the visual field at compelling the incongruous association to deliver, almost startlingly to ejaculate, the congruous, completing image: e.g., in the poem about the pine tree called "The Monkey Puzzle,"—"It knows that if a nomad may have dignity, Gibraltar has had more"; "the lion's ferocious chrysanthemum head seeming kind in comparison"; and "This porcupine-quilled, complicated starkness." The same effect is seen with greater scope in the first stanza of "The Steeple-Jack."

> Dürer would have seen a reason for living
>> in a town like this, with eight stranded whales
> to look at; with the sweet sea air coming into your house
> on a fine day, from water etched
>> with waves as formal as the scales
> on a fish.

Here the incongruity works so well as perhaps to be imperceptible. The reader beholds the sea as it is for the poem, but also as it never was to a modern (or a sailor's) eye, with the strength and light of all he can remember of Dürer's water-etchings, formal and "right" as the scales on a fish. It is the same formal effect, the Dürer vision, that sets the continuing tone, as the moon sets the tide (with the sun's help), for the whole poem, bringing us in the end an emotion as clean, as ordered, as startling as the landscape which yields it.

> It could not be dangerous to be living
> > in a town like this, of simple people,
> who have a steeple-jack placing danger signs by the church
> while he is gilding the solid-
> > pointed star, which on a steeple
> stands for hope.

In "The Hero," which is complementary to "The Steeple-Jack" and with it makes "Part of a Novel, Part of a Poem, Part of a Play," [7] we have another type of association, on the intellectual plane, which *apparently* incongruous, is at heart surprising mainly because it is so exact. Some men, says Miss Moore, have been "lenient, looking upon a fellow creature's error with the feelings of a mother—a woman or a cat." The "cat" refines, selects and—removing the sentimental excess otherwise associated with "mother" in similar contexts—establishes the gesture and defines, in the apposition, the emotion. It is a similar recognition of identic themes in the apparently incongruous—though here the example is more normal to poetic usage—that leads to her defining statement about the Hero.

> > He's not out
> > seeing a sight but the rock
> > crystal thing to see—the startling **El Greco**
> > brimming with inner light—that
> > covets nothing that it has let go.

What Mr. Eliot puts into his Introduction about Miss Moore's exploitation of some of the less common uses of rhyme—besides stress-rhyme, rhyme against the metric, internal auditory rhyme, light rhyme—should excite the reader who has been oblivious to pursuit and the reader who has been aware to perusal. Here let us merely re-enforce Mr. Eliot with an example or so, and half an addition to his categories.

In the stanza from "The Hero" just quoted there is the paradigm for a rhyme-sound refrain which the well-memoried ear can catch. The first and last two lines of this and every other stanza rhyme on the sound of long "o," some light and some heavy. It is a question whether devices of this order integrally affect the poem in which they occur. If they do affect it, it must be in a manner that can neither be named nor understood, suffusing the texture unascertainably. But such devices do not need to be justified as integrating forces. It is enough for appreciation that this example should set up, as it does, a parallel music to the strict music of the poem which cannot be re-

---

[7] Something a hasty reader might miss is that (page 2, bottom) the Steeple-Jack, so orderly in his peril, might be part of a novel, and that the frock-coated Negro (page 5, top) might, with his sense of mystery, be part of a play. The text is "part of a poem." Miss Moore's titles are often the most elusive parts of her poems.

moved from it once it is there any more than it can be surely brought into it. It is part of the poem's weather. The Provençal poets worked largely in this order of rhyme, and in our own day Wallace Stevens has experimented with it.

Although many of the poems are made on intricate schemes of paired and delayed rhymes—there being perhaps no poem entirely faithful to the simple quatrain, heroic, or couplet structure—I think of no poem which for its rhymes is so admirable and so alluring as "Nine Nectarines and Other Porcelain." Granting that the reader employs a more analytical pronunciation in certain instances, there is in the last distich of each stanza a rhyme half concealed and half overt. These as they are first noticed perhaps annoy and seem, like the sudden variations, trills, mordents and turns in a Bach fugue, to distract from the theme, and so, later, to the collected ear, seem all the more to enhance it, when the pleasure that may be taken in them for themselves is all the greater. More precisely, if there be any ears too dull, Miss Moore rhymes the penultimate syllable of one line with the ultimate syllable of the next. The effect is of course cumulative; but the cumulus is of delicacy not mass; it is cumulative, I mean, in that in certain stanzas there would be no rhyme did not the precedent pattern make it audible. If we did not have

> a bat is winging. It
> is a moonlight scene, bringing. . . .

we should probably not hear

> and sets of Precious Things
> dare to be conspicuous.

What must be remembered is that anyone can arrange syllables, the thing is to arrange syllables at the same time you write a poem, and to arrange them as Miss Moore does, on four or five different planes at once. Here we emphasize mastery on the plane of rhyme. But this mastery, this intricacy, would be worthless did the poem happen to be trash.

Leaving the technical plane—at least in the ordinary sense of that term—there is another order of facts no less beguiling, the facts of what Miss Moore writes about—an order which has of course been touched on obliquely all along. What we say now must be really as oblique as before, no matter what the immediacy of approach; there is no meeting Miss Moore face to face in the forest of her poems and saying This is she, this is what she means and is: tautology is not the right snare for her or any part of her. The business of her poetry (which for us is herself) is to set things themselves delicately conceived in relations so fine and so accurate that their qualities, mutually stirred, will produce a new relation: an emotion. Her poems answer the question, What will happen in poetry, what emotion will transpire, when these things have been known or felt beside each other? The things are words and have qualities that may be called on apart from the qualities of the objects they name or connect. Keats's odes are composed on the same method, and Milton's *Lycidas.* But there are differences which must be mastered before the identity can be seen.

For Keats the Nightingale was a touchstone and a liberating symbol; it let him pour himself forth and it gave him a free symbol under which to subsume his images and emotions; the nightingale was a good peg of metonymy, almost, when he was done, a good synechdoche. For his purposes, the fact that he had a nightingale to preside over his poem gave the poem a suffusing order; and in the end everything flows into the nightingale.

With Miss Moore, in such poems as "An Octopus," "England," "The Labours of Hercules," "The Monkeys," and "The Plumet Basilisk," there is less a freeing of emotions and images under the aegis of the title notion, than there is a deliberate delineation of specific poetic emotions with the title notion as a starting point or spur: a spur to develop, compare, entangle, and put beside the title notion a series of other notions, which may be seen partly for their own sakes in passing, but more for what the juxtapositions conspire to produce. Keats's emotions were expansive and general but given a definite symbolic form; Miss Moore's emotions are special and specific, producing something almost a contraction of the given material, and so are themselves their own symbols. The distinction is exaggerated, but once seized the reader can bring it down to earth. Put another way, it is comparatively easy to say what Keats's poem is about, or what it is about in different places: it is about death and love and nostalgia, and about them in ways which it is enough to mention to understand. It is not easy to say what one of Miss Moore's longer poems is about, either as a whole or in places. The difficulty is not because we do not know but precisely because we do know, far more perfectly and far more specifically than we know anything about Keats's poem. What it is about is what it does, and not at any one place but all along. The parts stir each other up (where Keats put stirring things in sequence) and the aura of agitation resulting, profound or light as it may be, is what it is about. Naturally, then, in attempting to explain one of these poems you find yourself reading it through several times, so as not to be lost in it and so that the parts will not only follow one another as they must, being words, but will also be beside one another as their purpose requires them to be. This perhaps is why Miss Moore could write of literature as a phase of life: "If one is afraid of it, the situation is irremediable; if one approaches it familiarly what one says of it is worthless."

It is a method not a formula; it can be emulated not imitated; for it is the consequence of a radical leaning, of more than a leaning an essential trope of the mind: the forward stress to proceed, at any point, to proceed from one thing to another, crossing all gaps regardless, but keeping them all in mind. The poem called "The Monkeys" (in earlier versions "My Apish Cousins") has monkeys in the first line only. We proceed at once to "zebras supreme in their abnormality," and "elephants with their fog-coloured skin"; proceed, that is, with an abstract attribution and a beautifully innervated visual image. But the monkeys were not there for nothing; they signify the zoo and they establish an air for the poem that blows through it taking up a burden, like seeds, as it passes. I cannot say how the monkeys perform their function. But if it could be told it would not help; no more than it helps to say that the poem is composed not only on a rhyme and a typographic but also on a rigidly syllabic pattern. The first line of each stanza has fifteen syllables and the second sixteen; the third lines have ten, and the last, with which they balance, ten; and the fifth lines, except in the third stanza with thirteen, have fifteen. The fact of syllabic pattern has a kind of tacit interest, but we cannot say whether we can appreciate it, because we do not know whether even the trained ear can catch the weight of variations of this order. The monkeys are in a different position, and even if we cannot say in blueprint words what it is, we know that the interest is functional because we can report the fact of its experience.

More could be said—and in description a poem merely difficult and complex enough to require deep and delicately adjusted attention might seem a labyrinth; but let us rather move to a different poem, "An Octopus," and there select for emphasis a different aspect of the same method. This is a poem, if you like, about the Rocky Mountain Parks, Peaks, Fauna, and Flora; it is also about the Greek mind and language, and a great deal else. It contains material drawn from illustrated magazines, travel books, Cardinal Newman, Trollope, Richard Baxter's *The Saint's Everlasting Rest* (a book used in a dozen poems), W. D. Hyde's *Five Great Philosophies*, the Department of the Interior Rules and Regulations, and a remark overheard at the circus. Composed in free rhythm, natural cadence, and lines terminated by the criteria of conversational or rhetorical sense, it has a resemblance in form and typical content to certain of the Cantos of Ezra Pound; a resemblance strong enough to suggest that Pound may have partly derived his method from Miss Moore. The dates do not make derivation impossible, and the changes in structure from the earlier to the later Cantos confirm the suggestion. The pity in that case is that Pound did not benefit more; for there is a wide difference in the level and value of the effects secured. The elements in Pound's Cantos, especially the later ones, remain as I have argued elsewhere essentially disjunct because the substance of them is insufficiently present in the text; whereas in Miss Moore's poems of a similar order, and especially in "An Octopus," although themselves disjunct and even inviolate, coming from different countries of the mind, the substances are yet sufficiently present in the poem to compel conspiracy and co-operation. You cannot look in the words of a poem and see two objects really side by side without seeing a third thing, which will be specific and unique. The test, if reference can again be made to "Poetry," is in the genuineness of the presentation of the elements:[8] there must be real toads in the imaginary garden. Miss Moore has a habit of installing her esthetics in her poems as she goes along, and in "An Octopus" she pleads for neatness of finish and relentless accuracy, both in mountains and in literature; and the mountain has also, what literature ought to have and Miss Moore does have, a capacity for fact. These notions only refine the notion of the letter of the imagination. The point here is that the notions about the treatment of detail explain why Pound's later Cantos seem diffuse in character and intangible in import and why Miss Moore's poem has a unity that grows with intimacy.

There are more aspects of Miss Moore's method as there are other lights in which to see it, but enough has been touched on here to show what the method is like, that it is not only pervasive but integral to her work. It is integral to the degree that, with her sensibility being what it is, it imposes limits more profoundly than it liberates poetic energy. And here is one reason—for those who like reasons—for the astonishing fact that none of Miss Moore's poems attempt to be major poetry, why she is content with smallness in fact so long as it suggests the great by implication. Major themes are not susceptible of expression through a method of which it is the virtue to produce the idiosyncratic in the fine and strict sense of that word. Major themes, by definition of general and predominant interest, require for expression a method which produces the general in terms not of the idiosyncratic but the specific, and require, too, a form which seems to *contain* even more than to *imply* the wholeness beneath. The first poem in the present collection, "Part of a Novel, Part of a Poem, Part of a Play," comes as near to major expression as her method makes possible; and it is notable that here both the method and the content are more nearly "normal" than we are used to find. Elsewhere, though the successful poems achieve their established purposes, her method and her sensibility, combined, transform her themes from the normal to the idiosyncratic plane. The poem "Marriage," an excellent poem, is never concerned with either love or lust, but with something else, perhaps no less valuable, but certainly, in a profound sense, less complete.

[8] Mr. Eliot in his Introduction and Mr. Kenneth Burke in a review agree in finding genuineness paramount in Miss Moore's work.

Method and sensibility ought never, in the consideration of a poet, to be kept long separate, since the one is but the agent of growth and the recording instrument of the other. It is impossible to ascertain the stress of sensibility within the individual and it is an injustice to make the attempt; but it is possible to make at least indications of the sensibility informing that objective thing a body of poetry. Our last observation, that there is in the poem "Marriage" no element of sex or lust, is one indication. There is no sex anywhere in her poetry. No poet has been so chaste; but it is not the chastity that rises from an awareness—healthy or morbid—of the flesh, it is a special chastity aside from the flesh—a purity by birth and from the void. There is thus, by parallel, no contact by disgust in her work, but rather the expression of a cultivated distaste; and this is indeed appropriate, for within the context of purity disgust would be out of order. Following the same train, it may be observed that of all the hundreds of quotations and references in her poems none is in itself stirring, although some are about stirring things; and in this she is the opposite of Eliot, who as a rule quotes the thing in itself stirring; and here again her practice is correct. Since her effects are obtained partly by understatement, partly by ornament, and certainly largely by special emphasis on the quiet and the quotidian, it is clear that to use the thing obviously stirring would be to import a sore thumb, and the "great" line would merely put the poem off its track. Lastly, in this train, and to begin another, although she refers eulogistically many times to the dazzling color, vivid strength, and torrential flow of Hebrew poetry, the tone of her references is quiet and conversational.

By another approach we reach the same conclusion, not yet named. Miss Moore writes about animals, large and small, with an intense detached intimacy others might use in writing of the entanglements of people. She writes about animals as if they were people minus the soilure of overweeningly human preoccupations, to find human qualities freed and uncommitted. Compare her animal poems with those of D. H. Lawrence. In Lawrence you feel you have touched the plasm; in Miss Moore you feel you have escaped and come on the idea. The other life is there, but it is round the corner, not so much taken for granted as obliviated, not allowed to transpire, or if so only in the light ease of conversation: as we talk about famine in the Orient in discounting words that know all the time that it *might* be met face to face. In Miss Moore life is remote (life as good *and* evil) and everything is done to keep it remote; it is reality removed, but it is nonetheless reality, because we *know* that it is removed. This is perhaps another way of putting Kenneth Burke's hypothesis: "if she were discussing the newest model of automobile, I think she could somehow contrive to suggest an antiquarian's interest." Let us say that everything she gives is minutely precise, immediately accurate to the witnessing eye, but that both the reality under her poems and the reality produced by them have a nostalgic quality, a hauntedness, that cannot be reached, and perhaps could not be borne, by these poems, if it were.

Yet remembering that as I think her poems are expedient forms for ecstasies apprehended, and remembering, too, both the tradition of romantic reticence she observes and the fastidious thirst for detail, how could her poems be otherwise, or more? Her sensibility—the deeper it is the more persuaded it cannot give itself away—predicted her poetic method; and the defect of her method, in its turn, only represents the idiosyncrasy of her sensibility: that it, like its subject matter, constitutes the perfection of standing aside.

It is provisionally worth noting that Miss Moore is not alone but characteristic in American literature. Poe, Hawthorne, Melville (in *Pierre*), Emily Dickinson, and Henry James, all—like Miss Moore— shared an excessive sophistication of surfaces and a passionate predilection for the genuine—though Poe was perhaps not interested in too much of the genuine; and all contrived to present the conviction of reality best by making it, in most readers' eyes, remote.

Motives and Motifs in the Poetry of Marianne Moore

by Kenneth Burke

In this essay we would characterize the substance of Miss Moore's work as a specific poetic strategy. And we would watch it for insights which the contemplation of it may give us into the ways of poetic and linguistic action generally. For this purpose we shall use both her recently published book, *What Are Years*, and her *Selected Poems*, published in 1935 with an introduction by T. S. Eliot (and including some work reprinted from an earlier volume, *Observations*).

On page 8 of the new book, Miss Moore writes:

> The power of the visible
> is the invisible;

and in keeping with the pattern, when recalling her former title, *Observations*, we might even have been justified in reading it as a deceptively technical synonym for "visions." One observes the visibles —but of the corresponding invisibles, one must be visionary. And while dealing much in things that can be empirically here, the poet reminds us that they may

> dramatize a
> meaning always missed
> by the externalist.

It is, then, a relation between external and internal, or visible and invisible, or background and personality, that her poems characteristically establish. Though her names for things are representative of attitudes, we could not say that the method is Symbolist. The objects exist too fully in their own right for us to treat them merely as objective words for subjects. T. S. Eliot says that her poetry "might be classified as 'descriptive' rather than 'lyrical' or 'dramatic.'" He cites an early poem that "suggests a slight influence of H. D., certainly

"Motives and Motifs in the Poetry of Marianne Moore." From *A Grammar of Motives* by Kenneth Burke (Englewood Cliffs: Prentice-Hall, Inc., 1945; Berkeley: University of California Press, 1969). Reprinted by permission of Prentice-Hall, Inc. First appeared in *Accent, II* (Spring 1942), 157–69. Several footnotes have been omitted for reasons of space.

of H. D. rather than of any other 'Imagist.'" And though asserting that "Miss Moore has no immediate poetic derivations," he seems to locate her work in the general vicinity of imagism, as when he writes:

> The aim of "imagism," so far as I understand it, or so far as it had any, was to introduce a peculiar concentration upon something visual, and to set in motion an expanding succession of concentric feelings. Some of Miss Moore's poems—for instance with animal or bird subjects— have a very good spread of association.

I think of William Carlos Williams. For though Williams differs much from Miss Moore in temperament and method, there is an important quality common to their modes of perception. It is what Williams has chosen to call by the trade name of "objectivist."

Symbolism, imagism, and objectivism would obviously merge into one another, since they are recipes all having the same ingredients but in different proportions. In symbolism, the subject is much stronger than the object as an organizing motive. That it, it is *what the images are symbolic of* that shapes their treatment. In imagism, there would ideally be an equality of the two motives, the subjective and objective. But in objectivism, though an object may be chosen for treatment because of its symbolic or subjective reference, once it has been chosen it is to be studied in its own right.

A man might become an electrician, for instance, because of some deep response to electricity as a symbol of power. Yet, once he had become an electrician and thus had converted his response to this subject into an objective knowledge of its laws and properties, he would thereafter treat electricity as he did, not because each of his acts as an electrician would be symbolic like his original choice of occupation, but because such acts were required by the peculiar nature of electricity. Similarly, a poet writing in an "objectivist" idiom might select his subject because of some secret or personal significance it has had for him; yet having selected it, he would find that its corresponding object had qualities to be featured and appraised for themselves. And he might pay so much attention to such appraisal that the treatment of the object would in effect "transcend" the motive behind its original singling-out.

Thus, the poem "Four Quartz Crystal Clocks" (in *What Are Years*) begins:

> There are four vibrators, the world's exactest clocks;
>   and these quartz time-pieces that tell
> time intervals to other clocks,
>   these workless clocks work well;
> and all four, independently the
>   same, are there in the cool Bell
>   Laboratory time

> vault. Checked by a comparator with Arlington
> they punctualize. . . .   (Etc.)

I think there would be no use in looking for "symbolist" or "imagist" motives behind the reference to the fact that precisely *four* clocks are mentioned here. It is an "objectivist" observation. We read of four, not because the number corresponds, for instance, to the Horsemen of the Apocalypse, but simply because there actually are four of them in the time vault. Similarly, "cool Bell Laboratory time vault" might have outlying suggestions of something like the coolness of a tomb—but primarily one feels that the description is there for purposes of objective statement; and had the nature of the scene itself dictated it, we should be reading of a "hot Bell Laboratory time tower." Though not journalism, it is reporting.

Yet any reader of Miss Moore's verse will quickly acknowledge that this theme, which provides an "objective" opportunity for the insertion of transitions between such words as "exactest," "punctualize," "careful timing," "clear ice," "instruments of truth," and "accuracy," is quite representative of her (and thus "symbolic" in the proportions of imagism). And the secondary level of the theme (its quality as being not the theme of clocks that tell the time, but of clocks that tell the time to clocks that tell the time)—I should consider thoroughly symbolic, as signalizing a concern not merely for the withinness of motives, but for the withinness-of-withinness of motives, the motives behind motives.

We can call Miss Moore "objectivist," then, only by taking away the epithet in part. For though many details in her work seem to get there purely out of her attempt to report and judge of a thing's intrinsic qualities, to make us feel its properties as accurately as possible, the fact remains that, after you have read several of her poems, you begin to discern a strict principle of selection motivating her appraisals.

In *Selected Poems,* for instance, consider the poem, "People's Surroundings," that gives us a catalogue of correspondence between various kinds of agents and the scenes related to their roles. The poet is concerned to feature, in a background, the details that are an objective portrait of the person to whose kind of action this background belongs. "A setting must not have the air of being one"—a proscription one can observe if he makes the setting the extension of those in it. Here are relationships among act, scene, and agent (I use the three terms central to the philosophy of drama embodied in Henry James's prefaces). And among these people who move "in their respective places," we read of

> . . . the acacia-like lady shivering at the touch of a hand,
> lost in a small collision of orchids—

        dyed quicksilver let fall
        to disappear like an obedient chameleon in fifty shades of mauve
            and amethyst.

Here, with person and ground merged as indistinguishably as in a
pointillist painting by Seurat, the items objectify a tentative mood we
encounter throughout Miss Moore's verses. The lines are like a miniature impression of her work in its entirety. And when, contemplating
a game of bowls, she writes, "I learn that we are precisians, not
citizens of Pompeii arrested in action / as a cross-section of one's
correspondence would seem to imply," she here "learns" what she is
forever learning, in her contemplation of animals and natural and
fabricated things, as she seeks to isolate, for her appreciation and our
own, the "great amount of poetry in unconscious fastidiousness."

I think appreciation is as strong a motive in her work as it was in
the work of Henry James. "The thing is to lodge somewhere at the
heart of one's complexity an irrepressible *appreciation*," he says in his
preface to *The Spoils of Poynton*. And: "To criticise is to appreciate,
to appropriate, to take intellectual possession, to establish in fine a
relation with the criticised thing and make it one's own." It is a kind
of private property available to everyone—and is perhaps the closest
secular equivalent to the religious motive of glorification. It is a form
of gratitude. And following out its possibilities, where one might
otherwise be querulous he can instead choose to be precise. This
redemption or transformation of complaint is, I think, essential to
the quality of perception in Miss Moore's verse. (Rather, it is an
anticipation of complaint: getting there first, it takes up all the room.)

In "Spencer's Ireland" (*What Are Years*), we may glimpse somewhat
how this redemption can take place. Beginning in a mood of appreciation almost studious, the poem ends

                The Irish say your trouble is their
            trouble and your
                    joy their joy? I wish
            I could believe it;
            I am troubled, I'm dissat-
                    isfied, I'm Irish.

Since it is towards this end that the poem is directed, we may assume
that from this end it derives the logic of its progression.

Note the general tenor of the other observations: on family, on marriage, on independence and yielding, on the freedom of those "made
captive by supreme belief." There is talk of enchantments, of trans-
formations, of a coat "like Venus' mantle lined with stars . . . the
sleeves new from disuse," of such discriminations as we get

> when large dainty
> fingers tremblingly divide the wings
> of the fly.

And there are lines naming birds, and having a verbal music most lovely in its flutter of internal rhymes:

> the guillemot
>   so neat and the hen
> of the heath and the
> linnet spinet-sweet.

All these details could be thought of as contextual to the poem's ending (for, if you single out one moment of a poem, all the other moments automatically become its context). If, then, we think of the final assertion as the act, we may think of the preceding contextual material as the scene, or background, of this act (a background that somehow contains the same quality as the act, saying implicitly what the act of the final assertion says explicitly). Viewed thus we see, as the underlying structure of this "description," a poem that, if treated as a lyric, would have somewhat the following argument: "Surrounded with details appropriate to my present mood, with a background of such items as go with matters to do with family, union, independence, I, an Irish girl (while the birds are about—and sweetly) am dissatisfied."

I won't insist that I'm not wrong. But in any case, that's the way I read it. And I would discern, behind her "objectivist" study and editorializing, what are essentially the lineaments of a lyric. But where the lyrist might set about to write, "In the moonlight, by the river, on a night like this in Spain," I can think of Miss Moore's distributing these items (discreetly and discretely) among conversational observations about the quality of light in general and moonlight in particular, about rivers mighty and tiny, in mountains, across plains, and emptying into the desert or the sea, about the various qualifications that apply to the transformation from twilight to darkness, in suburbs, or over bays, etc.; and from travel books of Spain we might get some bits that, pieced together, gave us all into which, in her opinion, the given night in Spain should be "broken down."

We might try from another angle by suggesting that Miss Moore makes "because" look like "and." That is, the orthodox lyrist might say, in effect, "I am sad *because* the birds are singing thus." A translation into Miss Moore's objectivist idiom would say in effect: "There are such and such birds—*and* birds sing thus and so—*and* I am sad." The scenic material would presumably be chosen because of its quality as objective replica of the subjective (as observed moments in the scene that correspond to observing moments in the agent). But even where they had been selected because of their bearing upon the plaint, her subsequent attention to them, with appreciation as a motive, would transform the result from a purely psychologistic rhetoric (the traditional romantic device of simply using scenic terms as a vocabulary for the sympathetic naming of personal moods). And the result would be, instead, an appraisal or judgment of many things in and for themselves. They would be encouraged to disclose their traits, not simply that they might exist through the vicarage of words, but that they might reveal their properties as workmanship (workmanship being a trait in which the ethical and the esthetic are one).

What are years? That is, if we were to assemble a thesaurus of all the important qualifications of the term "years" as Miss Moore uses it, what would these qualifications be? I suppose a title is always an assertion because it is a thing—and every thing is positive. Years, we learn by her opening poem of that title, are at least a quality of observation (vision), involving the obligation of courage, of commands laid upon the self to be strong, to see deep and be glad. And years possess the quality of one

> . . . who
> accedes to mortality
> and in his imprisonment, rises
> upon himself as
> the sea in a chasm. . . .

Who does this, we are told, "sees deep and is glad." Years are also, by the nature of the case, steps from something to something. And to indicate a curve of development from the earlier volume, we might recall this same theme (of the rising water) as it was treated previously. I refer to a poem, "Sojourn in the Whale," which, beginning on the theme, "Trying to open locked doors with a sword," had likewise talked of Ireland. It is addressed to "you," a "you" who has heard men say: "she will become wise and will be forced to give / in. Compelled by experience, she / will turn back; water seeks its own level." Whereat

> . . . you
> have smiled. 'Water in motion is far
> from level.' You have seen it, when obstacles happened to bar
> the path, rise automatically.

In the earlier poem, the figure was used defensively, even oppositionally. It is a tactic not common in Miss Moore's verse; as against the dialectician's morality of eristic, she shows a more feminine preference for the sheer ostracizing of the enemy, refuting by silence— disagreement implying the respect of intimacy, as in her poem on "Marriage," wittily appraising the "fight to be affectionate," she quotes, "No truth can be fully known until it has been tried by the tooth of disputation."

(When Miss Moore was editor of *The Dial*, her ideal number, as regards the reviews and articles of criticism, would I think have been one in which all good books got long favorable reviews, all middling books got short favorable reviews, and all books deserving of attack were allowed to go without mention. One can imagine how such a norm could be reached either charitably, through stress upon appreciation as motive, or not so charitably, by way of punishment, as when Miss Moore observes in "Spencer's Ireland": "Denunciations do not affect the culprit; nor blows, but it / is torture to him not to be spoken to." We need not decide between these motives in all cases, since they can comfortably work in unison.)

In contrast with the "oppositional" context qualifying the figure of the rising water in the earlier poem, "Sojourn in the Whale," its later variant has a context almost exaltedly positive. And repeating the same pattern (of affirmation in imprisonment) in another figure, the later poem widens the connotations of the years thus:

> . . . The very bird
> grown taller as he sings, steels
> his form straight up. Though he is captive
> his mighty singing
> says satisfaction is a lowly
> thing, how pure a thing is joy.
> This is mortality,
> this is eternity.

The pattern appears more conversationally (*What Are Years*, p. 12) in the suggestion that it must have been a "humorous" workman who made

> this greenish Waterford
> glass weight with the summit curled down toward
> itself as the
> grass grew,

and in "The Monkey Puzzle" (*Selected Poems*) we read

> its tail superimposed upon itself in a complacent half spiral,
> incidentally so witty.

Still, then, trying to discover what are years (or rather, what all are years), we might also recall, in *Selected Poems*, the poem on "The Fish," where the one fish featured as representative of its tribe is observed "opening and shutting itself like / an / injured fan"—in quality not unlike "The Student" of *What Are Years* who

> . . . is too reclusive for
> some things to seem to touch
> him, not because he
> has no feeling but because he has so much.

As the poem of "The Fish" develops, we might say that the theme is transferred "from the organism to the environment"; for we next read of a chasm through which the water has driven a wedge—and injury is here too, since

> All
> external
> marks of abuse are present on this
> defiant edifice.—

And finally

> Repeated
> evidence has proved that it can live
> on what cannot revive
> its youth. The sea grows old in it.

A chasm in the sea, then, becomes rather the sea in a chasm. And this notable reversal, that takes place in the areas of the "submerged," would also seem to be an aspect of "years." Which would mean that "years" subsume the synecdochic possibilities whereby those elements that cluster together can represent one another: here the active can become passive, the environed can become the environment, the container can be interchangeable with the contained. In possessing such attributes, "years" are poetry.

We may at this point recall our beginning—the citation concerning visible and invisible. In "The Plumet Basilisk" (*Selected Poems*) we read of this particular lizard that, "king with king,"

> He leaps and meets his
> likeness in the stream.

He is (in the poem it is a quotation)

> 'the ruler of Rivers, Lakes, and Seas,
> invisible or visible'—

and as scene appropriate to the agent, this basilisk is said to live in a basilica. (Another lizard, in the same poem, is said to be "conferring wings on what it grasps, as the airplant does"; and in "The Jerboa," we are told of "this small desert rat" that it "honours the sand by assuming its colour.") Likewise

> the plumet portrays
> mythology's wish
> to be interchangeably man and fish.

What I am trying to do, in reaching out for these various associations, is to get some comprehensive glimpse of the ways in which the one pervasive quality of motivation is modified and ramified. I am trying, in necessarily tenuous material, to indicate how the avowed relation between the visible and the invisible finds variants, or sophistications, in "objectivist" appreciation; how this appreciation, in an age of much querulousness, serves rather to transcend the querulous (*Selected Poems*, p. 34: "The staff, the bag, the feigned inconsequence / of manner, best bespeak that weapon, self-protectiveness"); and how this same pattern takes form in the theme of submergence, with its interchangeabilities, and so in the theme of water rising on itself. At another point the motive takes as its object the motif of the spinster ("You have been compelled by hags to spin / gold thread from straw," with incidental suggestions of esthetic alchemy, lines that appear in "Sojourn in the Whale," and so link with submergence, Ireland, and the theme of spirited feminine independence, thus relating to kindred subjects in the later poem, "Spenser's Ireland"). I have also suggested that a like quality of imagination is to be found in the intellectual ways of one who selects as his subject not clocks, but clocks for clocks. (To appreciate just what goes on here, one might contrast these contemplative clocks—serene in their role as the motives behind motives—with the ominous clock-faces of Verhaeren, or in the grotesque plays of Edmund Wilson, which no one seems to have read but me.) From these crystal clocks, I could then advance to another variant, as revealed in the treatment of ice and glass. These would, I think, be animated by the same spirit. See for instance (in *Selected Poems*) the study of the glacier as "an octopus of ice":

> this fossil flower concise without a shiver,
> intact when it is cut,
> damned for its sacrosanct remoteness.

"Relentless accuracy is the nature of this octopus / with its capacity for fact"—which would make it a glacier with an objectivist esthetic. And two levels of motive are figured in the splendid concluding vista of

> . . . the hard mountain 'planed by ice and polished by the wind'—
> the white volcano with no weather side;
> the lightning flashing at its base,
> rain falling in the valleys, and snow falling on the peak—.[1]

[1] This is cited from the poem that follows the one on "Marriage," and is in turn followed by "Sea Unicorns and Land Unicorns." The three could be taken together as a triptych that superbly illustrates three stages in the development of one idea. First, we have the subtly averse poem on marriage (done in a spirit of

We might have managed more easily by simply demarcating several themes, like naming the different ingredients that go to make up a dish. Or as with the planks that are brought together, to make a campaign platform, regardless of their fit with one another. But the relation among the themes of a genuine poetry is not of this sort. It is *substantial*—which is to say that all the branches spread from a single trunk.

I am trying to suggest that, without this initial substantiality, "objectivism" would lead not to the "feigned inconsequence of manner" that Miss Moore has mastered, but to inconsequence pure and simple. But because of this substantiality, the surfaces are derived from depth; indeed, the strict lawfulness in their choice of surfaces is depth. And the objects treated have the property not simply of things, but of volitions. They derive their poignancy as motifs from their relation to the sources of motive. And the relation between observer and observed is not that of news and reporter, but of "conversities" (her word).

In the earlier volume there is a poem, "Black Earth," wherein surprisingly the poet establishes so close an identification with her theme as not merely to "observe" it with sympathy and appreciation, but to speak for it. This is one of her rare "I" poems—and in it the elephant sometimes speaks with the challenge and confidence of an Invictus. Beginning on the theme of emergence (coupled with delight in the thought of submergence at will), there is first a celebration of the sturdy skin; then talk of power ("my back is full of the history of power"); and then: "My soul shall never be cut into / by a wooden spear." Next comes mention of the trunk, and of poise. And interwoven with the vigor of assertion, the focal theme is there likewise:

---

high comedy that portrays marital quarrelings as interrelated somewhat like the steps of a minuet). Then comes the precise yet exalted contemplation of the glacier. And finally a discussion of the unicorn, a legendary solitaire:

> Thus this strange animal with its miraculous elusiveness,
> has come to be unique,
> 'impossible to take alive',
> tamed only by a lady inoffensive like itself—
> as curiously wild and gentle.

And typically, she cites of it that, since lions and unicorns are arch enemies, and "where the one is the other cannot be missing," Sir John Hawkins deduced an abundance of lions in Florida from the presence of unicorns there.

The theme of the lightning that flashes at the base of the glacier is varied in the unicorn poem (in a reference to "the dogs / which are dismayed by the chain lightning / playing at them from its horn"). And it is varied also in a poem on the elephant (still to be discussed) that

> has looked at the electricity and at the earth-
> quake and is still
> here; . . .

> that tree-trunk without
> roots, accustomed to shout
>> its own thoughts to itself . . .

and:

>> . . . The I of each is to
> the I of each
> a kind of fretful speech
>> which sets a limit on itself; the elephant is
>> black earth preceded by a tendril?

I think we can make a point by recalling this earlier poem when, in "Smooth Gnarled Crape Myrtle" (*What Are Years*), the theme of the elephant's trunk appears again, this time but in passing, contextual and "tangential" to the themes of birds, union, loneliness:

>> . . . 'joined in
> friendship, crowned by love.'
> An aspect may deceive; as the
> elephant's columbine-tubed trunk
> held waveringly out—
> an at will heavy thing—is
> delicate.

Surely, "an at will heavy thing" is a remarkable find. But one does not make such observation by merely looking at an elephant's trunk. There must have been much to discard. In this instance, we can know something about the omissions, quite as though we had inspected earlier drafts of the poem with their record of revisions. For though a usage in any given poem is a finished thing, and thus brilliant with surface, it becomes in effect but "work in progress" when we align it with kindred usages (emergent, fully developed, or retrospectively condensed) in other poems. And here, by referring to "Black Earth," we can find what lies behind the reference to the elephant's trunk in "Smooth Gnarled Crape Myrtle." We can know it for a fact what kind of connotations must, for the poet, have been implicit in the second, condensed usage. Hence we can appreciate the motives that enabled this trunk to be seen not merely as a *thing*, but as an *act*, representative of the assertion in "Black Earth." And by reviewing the earlier usage we can know the kind of volitional material which, implicit in the later usage, led beyond the perception of the trunk as a thing to this perception of it as an act. At such moments, I should say, out of our idealistic trammels we get a glimpse of realism in its purity. For as materialism is a stress upon the scene, idealism a stress upon the agent, mysticism a stress upon the purpose, and pragmatism a stress upon the means or agency, so realism is complete when it enables us to see in terms of the act.

Or let us look at another instance. Sensitivity in the selection of words resides in the ability, or necessity, to feel behind the given word a history—not a past history, but a future one. Within the word, collapsed into its simultaneous oneness, there is implicit a sequence, a complexity of possible narratives that could be drawn from it. If you would remember what words are in this respect, and how in the simultaneity of a word histories are implicit, recall the old pleasantry of asking someone, "What's an accordion," whereat invariably as he explains he will start pumping a bellows.

Well, among Miss Moore's many poems enunciating aspects of her esthetic credo, or commenting on literary doctrines and methods, there is one, "To a Snail," beginning:

> If 'compression is the first grace of style',
> you have it. Contractility is a virtue
> as modesty is a virtue.

And this equating of an esthetic value with a moral one is summed up by locating the principle of style "in the curious phenomenon of your occipital horn."

In her poem on the butterfly (*What Are Years*, p. 17), the mood of tentativeness that had been compressed within the term "contractility" reveals its significant narrative equivalents. As befits the tentative, or contractile, it is a poem of jeopardy, tracing a tenuous relationship between a butterfly ("half deity half worm," "last of the elves") and a nymph ("dressed in Wedgwood blue"), with light winds (even a "zephyr") to figure the motives of passion. Were not the course of a butterfly so intrinsically akin to the "inconsequential ease" and "droverlike tenacity" of Miss Moore's own versa-tilities, one might not have much hope for a poem built about this theme (reminiscent of many musical Papillons—perhaps more than a theme, perhaps a set idiom, almost a form). Here, with the minute accuracy of sheerly "objectivist" description, there is a subtle dialectic of giving and receiving, of fascinations and releases—an interchange of delicately shaded attitudes. In this realm, things reached for will evade, but will follow the hand as it recedes.

Through the tracery of flight, there are two striking moments of stasis, each the termination of a course: one when "the butterfly's tobacco-brown unglazed / china eyes and furry countenance confront / the nymph's large eyes"—and the second when, having broken contact with the nymph's "controlled agitated glance," the "fiery tiger-horse" (at rest, but poised against the wind, "chest arching / bravely out") is motivated purely by relation to the zephyr alone. The poem concludes by observing that this "talk" between the animal and the zephyr "was as strange as my grandmother's muff."

I have called it a poem of jeopardy. (When butterfly and nymph

confront each other, "It is Goya's scene of the tame magpie faced /
by crouching cats.") It is also a poem of coquetry (perhaps our last
poem of coquetry, quite as this butterfly was the last of the elves—
coquetry now usually being understood as something that comes
down like a ton of brick).

The tentativeness, contractility, acquires more purely the theme
of jeopardy in 'Bird-Witted" (*What Are Years*), reciting the incident
of the "three large fledgling mocking-birds," awaiting "their no longer
larger mother," while there approaches

> the
> intellectual cautious-
> ly c r e e p ing cat.

If her animals are selected for their "fastidiousness," their fastidiousness itself is an aspect of contractility, of jeopardy. "The Pangolin" (*What Are Years*), a poem which takes us through odd noctur-
nal journeys to the joyous saluting of the dawn, begins: "Another
armoured animal"—and of a sudden you realize that Miss Moore's
recondite menagerie is almost a thesaurus of protectivenesses. Thus
also, the poem in which occur the lines anent visible and invisible,
has as its conclusion:

> unsolicitude having swallowed up
> all giant birds but an
> alert gargantuan
> little-winged, magnificently
> speedy running-bird. This one
> remaining rebel
> is the sparrow-camel.

The tentativeness also manifests itself at times in a cult of rarity,
a collector's or antiquarian interest in the present, a kind of stylistic
tourism. And it may lead to a sheer word play, of graduated sort (a
Laforguian delight in showing how the pedantries can be reclaimed
for poetry):

> The lemur-student can see
> that the aye-aye is not
>
> an angwan-tibo, potto, or loris.

Yet mention of the "aepyornis" may suggest the answer we might
have given, were we up on such matters, to one who, pencil in hand
and with the newspaper folded to make it firmer, had asked, "What's
a gigantic bird, found fossil in Madagascar in nine letters?" As for
her invention, "invis   ible," I can't see it.

Tonally, the "contractility" reveals itself in the great agility, even restlessness, which Miss Moore imparts to her poetry by assonance, internal rhyme, and her many variants of the run-over line. We should also note those sudden nodules of sound which are scattered throughout her verses, such quick concentrations as "rude root cudgel," "the raised device reversed," "trim trio on the tree-stem," "furled fringed frill," or tonal episodes more sustained and complex, as the lines on the birds in Ireland (already quoted), or the title, "Walking-Sticks and Paper-Weights and Water-Marks," or

> . . . the redbird
> the red-coated musketeer,
> the trumpet-flower, the cavalier,
> the parson, and the
> wild parishoner. A deer-
> track in a church-floor
> brick . . .

One noticeable difference between the later selection and the earlier one is omission of poems on method. In *Selected Poems* there were a great many such. I think for instance of: "Poetry," containing her ingenious conceit, "imaginary gardens with real toads in them"; "Critics and Connoisseurs"; "The Monkeys"; "In the Days of Prismatic Colour"; "Picking and Choosing"; "When I Buy Pictures"; "Novices" (on action in language, and developed in imagery of the sea); "The Past is the Present" ("ecstasy affords / the occasion and expediency determines the form"); and one which propounds a doctrine as its title: "In This Age of Hard Trying, Nonchalance is Good and."

But though methodological pronouncements of this sort have dropped away, in the closing poem on "The Paper Nautilus," the theme does reappear. Yet in an almost startlingly deepened transformation. Here, proclaiming the poet's attachment to the poem, there are likenesses to the maternal attachment to the young. And the themes of bondage and freedom (as with one "hindered to succeed") are fiercely and flashingly merged.

On Being Modern with Distinction

by John Crowe Ransom

Miss Moore's verse is so fine that its reception has been difficult and, I am persuaded, even yet is rare. And it is revolutionary. One likes to hope for any reader that its brilliance will finally be rewarding. But meanwhile its effect upon a reluctant modern, whether he be a poet or a mere reader, may be rather painful because it shakes the foundations of his comfortable assurance of what poetry should be. In her art she occupies a position somewhat like that which Debussy used to assume for us in music. She is a modern artist; and her modernity is fluent and authoritative, not easy to brush aside. Nevertheless, modernity comes to us painfully, if it is radical, and at some cost.

Original as Miss Moore is, our faith in the sequential order of history will not allow us to fail to look for derivations. We sense in her a break with the poetic style-book that has done service for so long, but we would identify the precise moment of her discontinuity and so at least reduce it to its minimum. I will therefore record my own impression that she is one of the consequences, and up to now the handsomest consequence, of the Imagist cult of thirty years ago. The great break was made there.

The ambition of the Imagists was, no doubt, to expel from their verse some of those effects which belonged most officially within the appointments of poetry. Among these they abhorred the heaviness in the metrical accents; the sacerdotal approach to the theme; and the metaphorical and hyperbolical turn of language with which poetic discourse seemed determined to envelop itself as with an atmosphere of the supernatural. The Imagists were prepared to secularize or de-solemnize their verse, and to earn for it some of that sort of distinction that is conceded to a fine prose. But of course they were not equal to the performance of the poetry which they planned. Upon any one of them we may imagine that we should confer credit if we pro-

"On Being Modern With Distinction" by John Crowe Ransom. From *Quarterly Review of Literature*, 4, No. 2 (1948), 136–42. Copyright 1948 by *Quarterly Review of Literature*. Reprinted by permission of the author and *Quarterly Review of Literature*.

nounced the judgment that he or she was—a precursor to Miss Moore.

I have liked very much the general magnanimity of Mr. T. S. Eliot's tribute, in his Introduction to the *Selected Poems,* and of course I have profited by the several cues which he offers there to her subsequent critics. Now Mr. Eliot's own poetry is modern too; but I think it is agreed, to speak roughly, that his modernity is some variation of the Symbolist way of poetry. It works with the old effects, which are the true and tried ones, the technically "poetic"; but presents them in thick rich nodes of meaning, in cryptic involutions rather than periodic syntax, or, from the point of view of the rational consciousness, in condensations and over-determinations as the Freudians might say. Mr. Eliot is a major voyager on one stream of modernity with which we have a good acquaintance, but it is not the pellucid stream that Miss Moore is embarked upon.

I should wonder if Mr. Eliot does not do Miss Moore a disservice when he raises the question of the "greatness" of her work, even though he raises it provisionally as one to be answered finally by the judgment of generations later than her own generation. Greatness is something for the kind of poetry in which he practices, perhaps, but it would seem beyond the intention of her kind, and so foreign to it that if I am not mistaken she would be the first to repel the idea. For this reason: that in our judgment of personages and their accomplishments we attribute greatness to those that take their impulse out of more primitive or heroic occasions than she is concerned with.

Let us compare her kind of human interest with that, for example, of Marcus Cato, the countryman who had come into Rome and was proceeding to reform the society of the capital. Cato, observing how the moral fibre of Romans was softening, stood out for the old austerity of living, and spent himself dangerously both in person and in his office of Censor. If so intense an effort in so elemental a situation does not meet, as we read, with some ridiculous degree of unsuccess, we will cheerfully put Cato down as among the great. And as for Miss Moore, we feel that she accepts her own society scarcely more than Cato accepted his. But her effort is a subtler one, and it is not delivered in the public forum, nor pitched on the plane of the folk morality and the laws.

Chiefly, she makes public in her verse the exempla of rightness or of beauty that have hit her fastidious taste. They are remarkably various. Sometimes they are the obscurer members of the animal kingdom; or rather, they are that as likely as not, and so often that we must conceive her in part as a curious naturalist in the succession of Pliny the Elder. Or they may be objects in the human sort, such as exhibit themselves in the regions of men, the classes, and the trades; or the works of men, such as the objects of art and the paraphernalia of fine living, including the precision instruments—for high thinking in Miss Moore's understanding of things goes with fine prop-erties. I have no doubt that before long the knowledge of Miss Moore's poetry will be so diffused that graduate students will be listing her objects and occasions in shining categories. But these very special objects she is content merely to cite in their integrity as beautiful objects, or to furnish with a little commentary in the lightest of ac-cents. This "merely," however, may be misleading. As beautiful ob-jects they are conspicuously in their duty, for they impart the sense not only of the generous dispensations of prodigious nature, but of that responsive economic intelligence which is of the essence of being human, the very thing that common prudential discourse is fond of rendering with its gross precepts and its heavy emphases.

For these registrations of her world she has suitably delicate an-tennae. They reach to the limits of what is tangible, and beyond these they project her imaginatively and very surely into the world of her insatiable reading. But such is her fidelity that she is not afraid of the sheer and homely natural detail, as if she trusted that poetic illumination presently would rise even out of nature, even out of prose; as it does.

She is usually successful with her effects. But they are minor not major effects, in the degree of their remoteness from the primitive range of interest; it takes many of them to yield the full dimensions of this poet. Her critic is apt to feel that in decency he can never quote enough of her passages to make perfectly resonant for the ill-acquainted the sense of how much more she is than merely the mis-tress of a casual elegance, such as she may well have seemed to our first impression.

I will quote twice, and first to the length of a whole poem where she seems especially to resemble some late and quite superior member of the Imagist group. It is in free verse and has little formal character. And it is about the sea, and should be compared with Lord Byron's declamations on the topic if we would see how far she has come from the old sententious style.

A Grave

Man looking into the sea,
taking the view from those who have as much right to it as you have to it
     yourself,
it is human nature to stand in the middle of a thing,
but you cannot stand in the middle of this;
the sea has nothing to give but a well excavated grave.
The firs stand in a procession, each with an emerald turkey-foot at the top,
reserved as their contours, saying nothing;

repression, however, is not the most obvious characteristic of the sea;
the sea is a collector, quick to return a rapacious look.
There are others besides you who have worn that look—
whose expression is no longer a protest; the fish no longer investigate them
for their bones have not lasted:
men lower nets, unconscious of the fact that they are desecrating a grave,
and row quickly away—the blades of the oars
moving together like the feet of water-spiders as if there were no such thing
    as death.
The wrinkles progress upon themselves in a phalanx—beautiful under net-
    works of foam,
and fade breathlessly while the sea rustles in and out of the seaweed;
the birds swim through the air at top speed, emitting cat-calls as heretofore—
the tortoise-shell scourges about the feet of the cliffs, in motion beneath them;
and the ocean, under the pulsation of lighthouses and noise of bell-buoys,
advances as usual, looking as if it were not that ocean in which dropped
    things are bound to sink—
in which if they turn and twist, it is neither with volition nor consciousness.

The energy of movement in this poem does not flag. If it seems to take us in too many directions, I venture to suggest that so far as I am concerned the poet is observing how life is lived as it were over the abyss, and is to be contemplated *sub specie mortalitatis,* but not fearfully unless by the fearful, nor brashly except by the brash.

But for a specimen that is technically more advanced I quote from the ostrich-poem, "He 'Digesteth Harde Yron.'" The passage will consist in the last three of the eleven stanzas, and begins with a recital of some of the peculiar honors that have been paid to our bird.

> Six hundred ostrich-brains served
> at one banquet, the ostrich-plume-tipped tent
>   and desert spear, jewel-
>   gorgeous ugly egg-shell
> goblets, eight pairs of ostriches
> in harness, dramatize a
>   meaning always missed
>   by the externalist.
>
> The power of the visible
> is the invisible; as even where
>   no tree of freedom grows,
>   so-called brute courage knows.
> Heroism is exhausting, yet
> it contradicts a greed that
>   did not wisely spare
>   the harmless solitaire

or great auk in its grandeur;
unsolicitude having swallowed up
all giant birds but an
alert gargantuan
little-winged, magnificently
speedy running-bird. This one
remaining rebel
is the sparrow camel.

It is after we have responded perceptually and emotionally to this passage, with its many excellences, that we should undertake the responsibilities of the critic. We repeat the response, and weigh it.

The technical addition here is a daring one and prompts us presently to some speculations. In this stanza, which is uniform throughout the poem, Miss Moore employs a favorite strategy. She partly metrifies her language. Now we have a delicious feeling for the sudden formality which comes over the poem every moment or so with the indented rhyming couplets. We like a little formality if it does not involve us too deeply. We also appreciate, doubtless, the value of those effects in the phonetic dimension, suddenly asserted in a poem which might otherwise not particularly have solicited the ear. But there are items on the other side of the ledger. It is not to be believed for a moment that iambic rhythms and measured couplets can impose themselves upon a prose language without causing it to become other than prose. Even if they should not require that one letter be altered within one word—which is highly improbable—they alter our sense of the prose by the new formality they dictate to the reading. They recover for the time being the effect which we thought had been repudiated: the effect of its being a special, portentous, official occasion, a Sunday occasion so to speak, inimical to the fidelity of the objective reporter. And perhaps we shall fancy even that they infect slightly the free lines which jostle against the metered ones. Thus Miss Moore exposes her peculiar poetic virtue dangerously to temptation.

I tell of these misgivings humbly; I do not know whether I can offer testimony as to the receptivity of the perfect reader. I confess to the uncomfortable feeling sometimes that the brilliant Miss Moore seems to be trying to have it both ways, when a Roman streak in me alleges that not even Miss Moore is so privileged.

Let it be said quickly that Miss Moore's rhymes if not her iambics must be very nearly the most unobtrusive to be found in English verse. She always pairs off her rhyming lines by equal indentation, and it is likely that otherwise the rhyme might escape even the good reader's attention. If it be claimed that in this light way of rhyming she is merely being evasive—as if wanting her poetry to be *in* the corpus of standard style but not really *of* it—it may be replied that she rather is being witty, as if to mock the compulsiveness of rhyming when it does not affect her own freedom.

But there is no end to this. And if we are left finally with an unfinished problem as to the solidity of her achievement, we will assure ourselves that it has excellences enough.

About One of Marianne Moore's Poems

by *Wallace Stevens*

My purpose is to bring together one of Miss Moore's poems and a paper, "On Poetic Truth," by H. D. Lewis. The poem, "He 'Digesteth Harde Yron,' " has just been reprinted in the *Partisan Reader*. The paper is to be found in the July number (1946) of *Philosophy, the Journal of the British Institute of Philosophy* (Macmillan, London).

I

Mr. Lewis begins by saying that poetry has to do with reality in its most individual aspect. An isolated fact, cut loose from the universe, has no significance for the poet. It derives its significance from the reality to which it belongs. To see things in their true perspective, we require to draw very extensively upon experiences that are past. All that we see and hear is given a meaning in this way. There is in reality an aspect of individuality at which every form of rational explanation stops short. Now, in his *Euphues*, Lyly repeats the following bit of folk-lore:

> Let them both remember that the Estridge
> digesteth harde yron to preserve his health.

The "Estridge," then, is the subject of Miss Moore's poem. In the second stanza she says:

> This bird watches his chicks with
> a maternal concentration, after
>   he has sat on the eggs
>   at night six weeks, his legs
> their only weapon of defense.

"About One of Marianne Moore's Poems." From *The Necessary Angel* by Wallace Stevens. Copyright 1948 by Wallace Stevens. Reprinted by permission of Alfred A. Knopf, Inc. and Faber & Faber, Ltd. First appeared in *Quarterly Review of Literature*, IV, No. 2 (1948), 143–49.

The *Encyclopaedia Britannica* says of the ostrich:

> Extremely fleet of foot, when brought to bay the ostrich uses its strong
> legs with great effect. Several hens combine to lay their eggs in one
> nest, and on these the cock sits by night, while the females relieve one
> another by day.

Somehow, there is a difference between Miss Moore's bird and the
bird of the *Encyclopaedia*. This difference grows when she describes
her bird as

The friend

of hippotigers and wild

asses, it is as

though schooled by them he was

the best of the unflying

pegasi.

The difference signalizes a transition from one reality to another. It
is the reality of Miss Moore that is the individual reality. That of
the *Encyclopaedia* is the reality of isolated fact. Miss Moore's reality
is significant. An aesthetic integration is a reality.

Nowhere in the poem does she speak directly of the subject of
the poem by its name. She calls it "the camel-sparrow" and the "the
large sparrow Xenophon saw walking by a stream," "the bird,"
"quadruped-like bird" and

alert gargantuan

little-winged, magnificently

speedy running-bird.

This, too, marks a difference. To confront fact in its total bleakness
is for any poet a completely baffling experience. Reality is not the
thing but the aspect of the thing. At first reading, this poem has an
extraordinarily factual appearance. But it is, after all, an abstraction.
Mr. Lewis says that for Plato the only reality that mattered is exemplified best for us in the principles of mathematics. The aim of
our lives should be to draw ourselves away as much as possible from
the unsubstantial, fluctuating facts of the world about us and establish some communion with the objects which are apprehended by
thought and not sense. This was the source of Plato's asceticism. To
the extent that Miss Moore finds only allusion tolerable she shares
that asceticism. While she shares it she does so only as it may be necessary for her to do so in order to establish a particular reality or,
better, a reality of her own particulars: the "overt" reality of Mr.
Lewis. Take, for example, her particulars of the bird's egg. She says:

The egg piously shown

as Leda's very own

> from which Castor and Pollux hatched,
> was an ostrich-egg.

Again she speaks of

> jewel-
> gorgeous ugly egg-shell
> goblet.

It is obvious from these few quotations that Miss Moore has already found an individual reality in the ostrich and again in its egg. After all, it is the subject in poetry that releases the energy of the poet.

Mr. Lewis says that poetry has to do with matter that is foreign and alien. It is never familiar to us in the way in which Plato wished the conquests of the mind to be familiar. On the contrary its function, the need which it meets and which has to be met in some way in every age that is not to become decadent or barbarous, is precisely this contact with reality as it impinges upon us from outside, the sense that we can touch and feel a solid reality which does not wholly dissolve itself into the conceptions of our own minds. It is the individual and particular that does this. No fact is a bare fact, no individual fact is a universe in itself. Is not Miss Moore creating or finding and revealing some such reality in the stanza that follows?

> Six hundred ostrich-brains served
> at one banquet, the ostrich-plume-tipped tent
> and desert spear . . .
> eight pairs of ostriches
> in harness, dramatize a
> meaning always missed
> by the externalist.

Here the sparrow-camel is all pomp and ceremony, a part of justice of which it was not only the symbol, as Miss Moore says, but also the source of its panoply and the delicacy of its feasts; that is to say, a part of unprecedented experience.

Miss Moore's finical phraseology is an element in her procedure. These lines illustrate this:

> Although the aepyornis
> or roc that lives in Madagascar, and
> the moa are extinct

and

> Heroism is exhausting.

But what irrevocably detaches her from the *Encyclopaedia* is the irony of the following:

How
could he, prized for plumes and eggs and young, used
        even as a riding-
        beast, respect men hiding
actorlike in ostrich-skins, with
the right hand making the neck move
        as if alive and
        from a bag the left hand

    strewing grain, that ostriches
    might be decoyed and killed!

and the delighted observation of the following:

        whose comic duckling head on its
        great neck, revolves with compass-
                needle nervousness,
            when he stands guard, in S-

        like foragings as he is
        preening the down on his leaden-skinned back.

The gist of the poem is that the camel-sparrow has escaped the greed that has led to the extinction of other birds linked to it in size, by its solicitude for its own welfare and that of its chicks. Considering the great purposes that poetry must serve, the interest of the poem is not in its meaning but in this, that it illustrates the achieving of an individual reality. Mr. Lewis has some very agreeable things to say about meaning. He says that the extraction of a meaning from a poem and appraisement of it by rational standards of truth have mainly been due to enthusiasm for moral or religious truth. He protests against the abstraction of this content from the whole and appraisement of it by other than aesthetic standards. The "something said" is important, but it is important for the poem only in so far as the saying of that particular something in a special way is a revelation of reality. He says:

If I am right, the essence of art is insight of a special kind into reality.

Moreover, if he is right, the question as to Miss Moore's poem is not in respect to its meaning but in respect to its potency as a work of art. Does it make us so aware of the reality with which it is concerned, because of the poignancy and penetration of the poet, that it forces something upon our consciousness? The reality so imposed need not be a great reality.

Of course, if it does, it serves our purpose quite as certainly as a less modest poem would serve it. It is here, Mr. Lewis concludes, that the affinity of art and religion is most evident today. He says that both have to mediate for us a reality not ourselves and that this is what the poet does and that the supreme virtue here is humility, for the humble are they that move about the world with the lure of the real in their hearts. . . .

It is true that Mr. Lewis contemplates a reality adequate to the profound necessities of life today. But it is no less true that it is easier to try to recognize it or something like it or the possible beginnings of it than to achieve it on that scale. Thus, the field in poetry is as great as it is in anything else. Nothing illustrates this better and nothing illustrates the importance of poetry better than this possibility that within it there may yet be found a reality adequate to the profound necessities of life today or for that matter any day. Miss Moore's poem is an instance of method and is not an example beyond the scale intended by her. She may well say:

> Que ce n'est pas grand merveille de voir que l'Ostruche
> digére le fer, veu que les poulles n'en font pas moins.

For she is not a proud spirit. It may be that proud spirits love only the lion or the elephant with its howdah. Miss Moore, however, loves all animals, fierce or mild, ancient or modern. When she observes them she is transported into the presence of a recognizable reality, because, as it happens, she has the faculty of digesting the "harde yron" of appearance.

Marianne Moore (1948)

by William Carlos Williams

The magic name, Marianne Moore, has been among my most cherished possessions for nearly forty years, synonymous with much that I hold dearest to my heart. If this invites a definition of love it is something I do not intend to develop in this place. On the contrary I intend to describe, very briefly and indirectly, a talent.

It is a talent which diminishes the tom-toming on the hollow men of a wasteland to an irrelevant pitter-patter. Nothing is hollow or waste to the imagination of Marianne Moore.

How so slight a woman can so roar, like a secret Niagara, and with so gracious an inference, is one with all mysteries where strength masquerading as weakness—a woman, a frail woman—bewilders us. Miss Moore in constant attendance upon her mother the greater part of her life has lived as though she needed just that emphasis to point up the nature of her powers.

Marianne Moore (whom for no adequate reason I always associate in my mind with Marie Laurencin who may be the size of a horse for all I know) once expressed admiration of Mina Loy; that was in 1916, let us say. I think it was because Mina was wearing a leopard-skin coat at the time and Marianne had stood there with her mouth open looking at her.

Marianne had two cords, cables rather, of red hair coiled around her rather small cranium when I first saw her and was straight up and down like the two-by-fours of a building under construction. She would laugh with a gesture of withdrawal after making some able assertion as if you yourself had said it and she were agreeing with you.

A statement she would defend, I think, is that man essentially is very much like the other animals—or a ship coming in from the sea —or an empty snail-shell: but there's not much use saying a thing like that unless you can prove it.

Therefore Miss Moore has taken recourse to the mathematics of art. Picasso does no different: a portrait is a stratagem singularly related to a movement among the means of the craft. By making these operative, relationships become self-apparent—the animal lives with a human certainty. This is strangely worshipful. Nor does one always know against what one is defending oneself.

I saw yesterday what might roughly be referred to as a birthday card—made by some child a hundred or so years ago in, I think, Andover, Massachusetts. It was approximately three inches in its greatest dimension, formally framed in black, the mat inside the frame being of a particularly brilliant crimson velvet, a little on the cerise side and wholly undimmed by age. This enclosed a mounted bouquet of minute paper flowers upon the remnants of what had been several artificial little twigs among greenish blue leaves.

There were in all three identically shaped four-petaled flowers, one a faded blue, one pinkish and one white, perfectly flat as though punched out of tissue paper. At the bottom of the bouquet, placed loosely across the stems under the glass, was a slightly crumpled legend plainly printed on a narrow half-inch strip of white paper:

Walk on roses.

I never saw a more apt expression. Its size had no relation to the merits of its composition or execution.

I don't know what else to say of Marianne Moore—or rather I should like to talk on indefinitely about her, an endless research into those relationships which her poems, her use of the materials of poetry, connote. For I don't think there is a better poet writing in America today or one who touches so deftly so great a range of our thought.

This is the amazing thing about a good writer, he seems to make the world come toward him to brush against the spines of his shrub. So that in looking at some apparently small object one feels the swirl of great events.

What it is that gives us this sensation, this conviction, it is impossible to know but that it is the proof which the poem offers us there can be little doubt.

Her Shield

by Randall Jarrell

Miss Moore's poems judge what is said about them almost as much as poems can, so that even one's praise is hesitant, uncertain of its welcome. As her readers know, her father used to say, "The deepest feeling always shows itself in silence; / not in silence, but restraint"; and she herself has said, "If tributes cannot / be implicit, give me diatribes and the fragrance of iodine." Quotation is a tribute as near implicit as I can get; so I will quote where I can, and criticize where I can't. (My father used to say, "The deepest feeling always shows itself in scratches; / not in scratches, but in iodine.") And I have found one little hole through which to creep to criticism, Miss Moore's "If he must give an opinion it is permissible that the / critic should know what he likes." I know; and to have to give an opinion is to be human. Besides, I have never believed her father about feeling; "entire affection hateth nicer hands," as Spenser says, and I should hate to trust to "armour's undermining modesty / instead of innocent depravity." And that last quotation isn't Spenser.

It felt queer to see all over again this year, in English reviews of Miss Moore's *Collected Poems,* those sentences—sentences once so familiarly American—saying that she isn't a poet at all. I can understand how anyone looking into her book for the first time, and coming on an early passage like "Disbelief and conscious fastidiousness were the staple / ingredients in its / disinclination to move. Finally its hardihood was / not proof against its / proclivity to more fully appraise such bits / of food as the stream / bore counter to it," might make this mistake; but what goes on in the mind that experiences

> And Bluebeard's Tower above the coral-reefs,
> the magic mouse-trap closing on all points of the compass,
> capping like petrified surf the furious azure of the bay,
> where there is no dust, and life is like a lemon-leaf,
> a green piece of tough translucent parchment,

and, dissatisfied, decides that it is prose? Aren't these lines (ordinary enough lines for her) the work of someone even at first glance a poet, with the poet's immemorial power to make the things of this world seen and felt and living in words? And even if the rhythms were those of prose—these are not—wouldn't we rather have poetry in prose than prose in verse? I wouldn't trade *Prudence is a rich, ugly old maid courted by Incapacity* for some epics.

Nowadays, over here, Miss Moore wins all the awards there are; but it took several decades for what public there is to get used to her—she was, until very recently, read unreasonably little and praised reasonably much. Even the circumstances hindered. The dust-jacket of her *Collected Poems* says: "Since the former volumes are out of print many readers will now, for the first time, have the opportunity to own the treasure of her poetry." This *is* a felicitous way for a publishing firm to say that it has allowed to remain out of print, for many years, most of the poetry of one of the great living poets. Miss Moore's prose-seeming, matter-of-factly rhythmed syllabic verse, the odd look most of her poems have on the page (their unusual stanzaic patterns, their words divided at the ends of lines, give many of them a consciously, sometimes misleadingly experimental or modernist look), their almost ostentatious lack of transitions and explanations, the absence of romance and rhetoric, of acceptedly Poetic airs and properties, did most to keep conservative readers from liking her poetry. Her restraint, her lack—her wonderful lack—of arbitrary intensity or violence, of sweep and overwhelmingness and size, of cant, of sociological significance, and so on, made her unattractive both to some of the conservative readers of our age and to some of the advanced ones. Miss Moore was for a long time (in her own phrase about something else) "Like Henry James 'damned by the public for decorum,' / not decorum but restraint." She demands, "When I Buy Pictures," that the pictures "not wish to disarm anything." (Here I feel like begging for the pictures, in a wee voice: "Can't they be just a *little* disarming?" My tastes are less firmly classical.) The poems she made for herself were so careful never to wish to disarm anyone, to appeal to anyone's habitual responses and grosser instincts, to sweep anyone resistlessly away, that they seemed to most readers eccentrically but forbiddingly austere, so that the readers averted their faces from her calm, elegant, matter-of-fact face, so exactly moved and conscientiously unappealing as itself to seem averted. It was not the defects of her qualities but the qualities that made most of the public reluctant to accept her as more than a special case: her extraordinary discrimination, precision and restraint, the odd propriety of her imagination, her gifts of "natural promptness" (I use the phrase she found, but her own promptness is preternatural) —all these stood in her way and will go on standing in her way.

These people who *can't read modern poetry because it's so*—this or

that or the other—why can't they read "Propriety" or "The Mind is
an Enchanting Thing" or "What Are Years" or "Steeple-Jack"? Aren't
these plain-spoken, highly-formed, thoughtful, sincere, magnificently
expressive—the worthy continuation of a great tradition of English
poetry? Wouldn't the poet who wrote the "Horatian Ode" have been
delighted with them? Why should a grown-up, moderately intelligent
reader have any trouble with an early poem like, say, "New York"?
The words that follow the title, the first words of the poem, are
the savage's romance—here one stops and laughs shortly, as anybody
but a good New Yorker will. (Her remark about Brooklyn, "this city
of freckled / integrity," has a more ambiguous face.) She goes on,
by way of the fact that New York is the centre of the wholesale fur
trade, to the eighteenth century when furs were the link between
the Five Nations and Bath, between Natty Bumppo and the Trianon:

> It is a far cry from the 'queen full of jewels'
> and the beau with the muff,
> from the gilt coach shaped like a perfume-bottle,
> to the conjunction of the Monongahela and the Allegheny,
> and the scholastic philosophy of the wilderness
> to combat which one must stand outside and laugh
> since to go in is to be lost.

And she finishes by saying about America—truthfully, one thinks and
hopes—that "it is not the dime-novel exterior, / Niagara Falls, the
calico horses and the war-canoe" that matter, it is not the resources
and the know-how, "it is not the plunder, / but 'accessibility to experience.' "

The only way to combat a poem like this is to stand outside and
laugh—to go in is to be lost, and in delight; how can you say better,
more concretely and intelligently and imaginatively, what that long
central sentence says? Isn't the word *scholastic* worth some books? Of
course, if the eighteenth century and the frontier don't interest you,
if you've never read or thought anything about them, the poem will
seem to you uninteresting or incommunicative; but it is unreasonable
to blame the poet for that. In grammar school, bent over the geogra-
phy book, all of us lingered over the unexpected geometrical magnificence of "the conjunction of the Monongahela and the Allegheny,"
but none of the rest of us saw that it was part of a poem—our America was here around us, then, and we didn't know. And isn't the
conclusion of Miss Moore's poem the best and truest case that can be
made out for Americans?

It is most barbarously unjust to treat her (as some admiring critics
do) as what she is only when she parodies herself: a sort of museum
poet, an eccentric shut-in dealing in the collection, renovation, and
exhibition of precise exotic properties. For she is a lot more American

a writer (if to be an American is to be the heir, or heiress, of all the ages) than Thomas Wolfe or Erskine Caldwell or—but space fails me; she looks lovingly and knowingly at this "grassless / linksless [no longer], languageless country in which letters are written / not in Spanish, not in Greek, not in Latin, not in shorthand, / but in plain American which cats and dogs can read!" Doesn't one's heart reverberate to that last phrase "as to a trumpet"?

Miss Moore is one of the most perceptive of writers, sees extraordinarily—the words fit her particularly well because of the ambiguity that makes them refer both to sensation and intelligence. One reads, at random among lines one likes: *But we prove, we do not explain our birth;* reads about the pangolin *returning before sunrise; stepping in the moonlight, / on the moonlight peculiarly;* reads, *An aspect may deceive; as the / elephant's columbine-tubed trunk / held waveringly out— / an at will heavy thing—is / delicate. / Art is unfortunate. / One may be a blameless / bachelor, and it is but a / step to Congreve.* One relishes a fineness and strangeness and firmness of discrimination that one is not accustomed to, set forth with a lack of fuss that one is not accustomed to either; it is the exact opposite of all those novels which present, in the most verbose and elaborate of vocabularies, with the greatest and most obvious of pains, some complacently and irrelevantly Sensitive perceptions. How much has been left out, here! (One remembers Kipling's *A cut story is like a poked fire.*) What intelligence vibrates in the sounds, the rhythms, the pauses, in all the minute particulars that make up the body of the poem! The tone of Miss Moore's poems, often, is enough to give the reader great pleasure, since it is a tone of much wit and precision and intelligence, of irony and forbearance, of unusual moral penetration—is plainly the voice of a person of good taste and good sense and good will, of a genuinely human being. Because of the curious juxtaposition of curious particulars, most of the things that inhabit her poetry seem extraordinarily bright, exact, and there—just as unfamiliar colours, in unfamiliar combinations, seem impossibly vivid. She is *the* poet of the particular—or, when she fails, of the peculiar; and is also, in our time, *the* poet of general moral statement. Often, because of their exact seriousness of utterance, their complete individuality of embodiment, these generalizations of hers seem almost more particular than the particulars.

In some of her poems Miss Moore has discovered both a new sort of subject (a queer many-headed one) and a new sort of connection and structure for it, so that she has widened the scope of poetry; if poetry, like other organisms, wants to convert into itself everything there is, she has helped it to. She has shown us that the world is more poetic than we thought. She has a discriminating love of what others have seen and made and said, and has learned (like a burglar who marks everything that he has stolen with the owner's name, and then exhibits it in his stall in the marketplace) to make novel and beautiful use of such things in her own work, where they are sometimes set off by their surroundings, sometimes metamorphosed. But for Miss Moore I'd never have got to read about "the emerald's 'grasslamp glow,'" or about the Abbé Berlèse, who said, "In the camelliahouse there must be / no smoke from the stove, or dew on / the windows, lest the plants ail. . . . / mistakes are irreparable and nothing will avail," or about "our clasped hands that swear, 'By Peace / Plenty; as / by Wisdom, Peace,'" or about any of a thousand such things—so I feel as grateful to her memory as to a novelist's. Novelists are the most remembering of animals, but Miss Moore comes next. . . .

The change in Miss Moore's work, between her earliest and latest poems, is an attractive and favourable change. How much more modernist, special-case, dryly elevated and abstract, she was to begin with! "As for butterflies, I can hardly conceive / of one's attending upon you, but to question / the congruence of the complement is vain, if it exists." Butter not only wouldn't melt in this mouth, it wouldn't go in; one runs away, an urchin in the gutter and glad to be, murmuring: "The Queen of Spain *has* no legs." Or Miss Moore begins a poem, with melting grace: "If yellow betokens infidelity, / I am an infidel. / I could not bear a yellow rose ill will / Because books said that yellow boded ill, / White promised well." One's eyes widen; one sits the poet down in the porch swing, starts to go off to get her a glass of lemonade, and sees her metamorphosed before one's eyes into a new *Critique of Practical Reason,* feminine gender: for her next words are, "However, your particular possession, / The sense of privacy, / Indeed might deprecate / Offended ears, and need not tolerate / Effrontery." And that is all; the poem is over. Sometimes, in her early poems, she has not a tone but a manner, and a rather mannered manner at that—two or three such poems together seem a dry glittering expanse, i.e., a desert. But in her later work she often escapes entirely the vice most natural to her, this abstract, mannered, descriptive, consciously prosaic commentary (accompanied, usually, by a manneredness of leaving out all introductions and transitions and explanations, as if one could represent a stream by reproducing only the stepping-stones one crossed it on). As she says, compression is the first grace of style—is almost a defining characteristic of the poetry our age most admires; but such passages as those I am speaking of are not compressed—the time wasted on Being Abstract more than makes up for the time saved by leaving out. Looking at a poem like "What Are Years," we see how much her style has changed. And the changes in style represent a real change in the poet: when one is

struck by the poet's seriousness and directness and lack of manner—
by both her own individual excellence and by that anonymous excellence the best poets sometimes share—it is usually in one of the poems
written during the '30's and '40's. I am emphasizing this difference
too much, since even its existence is ignored, usually; but it is interesting what a different general impression the *Collected Poems* gives,
compared to the old *Selected Poems*. (Not that it wasn't wonderful
too.)

How often Miss Moore has written about Things (hers are aesthetic-
moral, not commercial-utilitarian—they persist and reassure); or
Plants (how can anything bad happen to a plant?); or Animals with
holes, a heavy defensive armament, or a massive and herbivorous
placidity superior to either the dangers or temptations of aggression.
The way of the little jerboa on the sands—at once true, beautiful,
and good—she understands; but the little shrew or weasel, that kills,
if it can, two or three dozen animals in a night? the little larvae
feeding on the still-living caterpillar their mother has paralysed for
them? Nature, in Miss Moore's poll of it, is overwhelmingly in favour
of morality; but the results were implicit in the sampling—like the
Literary Digest, she sent postcards to only the nicer animals. In these
poems the lion never eats Androcles—or anything else except a paste
of seeded rotten apples, the national diet of Erewhon; so that her
truthful and surprising phrase, *the lion's ferocious chrysanthemum
head,* may seem less surprising than it would for a wilder lion. Because so much of our own world is evil, she has transformed the Animal Kingdom, that amoral realm, into a realm of good; her consola-
tory, fabulous bestiary is more accurate than, but is almost as arranged
as any medieval one. We need it as much as she does, but how can
we help feeling that she relies, some of the time, too surely upon this
last version of pastoral? "You reassure me and people don't, except
when they are like you—but really they are always like you," the
poems say sometimes, to the beasts; and it is wonderful to have it
said so, and for a moment to forget, behind the animals of a darken-
ing landscape, their dark companions.

Some of the changes in Miss Moore's work can be considered in
terms of Armour. Queer terms, you say? They are hers, not mine:
a good deal of her poetry is specifically (and changingly) about armour, weapons, protection, places to hide; and she is not only conscious that this is so, but after a while writes poems about the fact
that it is so. As she says, "armour seems extra," but it isn't; and
when she writes about "another armoured animal," about another
"thing made graceful by adversities, conversities," she does so with
the sigh of someone who has come home. She asks whether a woman's
looks are weapons or scalpels; comments, looking out on a quiet town:
"It could scarcely be dangerous to be living / in a town like this";

says about a man's nonchalance: "his by- / play was more terrible in its effectiveness / than the fiercest frontal attack. / The staff, the bag, the feigned inconsequence / of manner, best bespeak that weapon, self-protectiveness." *That weapon, self-protectiveness!* The poet knows that morals are not "the memory of success that no longer succeeds," but a part of survival.

She writes: "As impassioned Handel / . . . never was known to have fallen in love, / the unconfiding frigate-bird hides / in the height and in the majestic / display of his art." If Handel (or the frigate-bird) had been less impassioned he wouldn't have hidden, and if his feelings had been less deep they'd have been expressed with less restraint, we are meant to feel; it was because he was so impassioned that he "never was known to have fallen in love," the poem almost says. And how much sisterly approval there is in that *unconfiding!* When a frigate-bird buys pictures, you can bet that the pictures "must not wish to disarm anything." (By being disarming we sometimes disarm others, but always disarm ourselves, lay ourselves open to rejection. But if we do not make ourselves disarming or appealing, everything can be a clear, creditable, take-it-or-leave-it affair, rejection is no longer rejection. Who would be such a fool as to make advances to his reader, advances which might end in rejection or, worse still, in acceptance?) Miss Moore spoke as she pleased, and did not care whether or not it pleased; mostly this made her firm and good and different, but sometimes it had its drawbacks.

She says of some armoured animals that they are "models of exactness." The association was natural: she thought of the animals as models and of the exactness as armour—and for such a writer, there was no armour like exactness, concision, irony. She wished to trust, as absolutely as she could, in flat laconic matter-of-factness, in the minimal statement, understatement: these earlier poems of hers approach as a limit a kind of ideal minimal statement, a truth thought of as underlying, prior to, all exaggeration and error; the poet has tried to strip or boil everything down to this point of hard, objective, absolute precision. But the most extreme precision leads inevitably to quotation; and quotation is armour and ambiguity and irony all at once—turtles are great quoters. Miss Moore leaves the stones she picks up carefully uncut, but places them in an unimaginably complicated and difficult setting, to sparkle under the Northern Lights of her continual irony. Nobody has ever been better at throwing away a line than this Miss Facing-Both-Ways, this La Rochefoucauld who has at last rid himself of La Rochefoucauld, and can disabusedly say about man:

> he loves himself so much,
> he can permit himself
> no rival in that love. . . .

and about woman:

Her Shield

one is not rich but poor
when one can always seem so right. . . .

and about both:

What can one do for them—
these savages
condemned to disaffect
all those who are not visionaries
alert to undertake the silly task
of making people noble?

All this is from "Marriage," the most ironic poem, surely, written
by man or woman; and one reads it with additional pleasure because
it was written by the woman who was later to say, so tenderly and
magically: "What is more precise than precision? Illusion."

Along with precision she loved difficulty. She said about James and
others: "It is the love of doing hard things / that rebuffed and wore
them out—a public out of sympathy with neatness. / Neatness of
finish! Neatness of finish!" Miss Moore almost despairs of us in one
poem, until she comes across some evidence which shows that, in
spite of everything, "we are precisionists"; and Santa Claus's reindeer,
in spite of cutwork ornaments and fur like eidelweiss, are still "rigor-
ists," so she names the poem that for them. How much she cares for
useless pains, difficulties undertaken for their own sake! Difficulty is
the chief technical principle of her poetry, almost. (For sureness of
execution, for originality of technical accomplishment, her poetry is
unsurpassed in our time; Auden says almost that, and the author of
"Under Sirius" ought to know. Some of her rhymes and rhythms
and phrases look quite undiscoverable.) Such unnecessary pains, such
fantastic difficulties! Yet with manners, arts, sports, hobbies, they
are always there—so perhaps they are necessary after all.

But some of her earlier poems do seem "averted into perfection."
You can't put the sea into a bottle unless you leave it open at the
end, and sometimes hers is closed at both ends, closed into one of
those crystal spheres inside which snowflakes are falling on to a tiny
house, the house where the poet lives—or says that she lives. Sometimes Miss Moore writes about armour and wears it, the most delicately chased, live-seeming scale-armour anybody ever put together:
armour hammered out of fern seed, woven from the silk of invisible

cloaks—for it is almost, though not quite, as invisible as it pretends to be, and is when most nearly invisible most nearly protecting. One is often conscious while reading the poetry, the earlier poetry especially, of a contained removed tone; of the cool precise untouchedness, untouchableness, of fastidious rectitude; of innate merits and their obligations, the obligations of ability and intelligence and aristocracy—for if aristocracy has always worn armour, it has also always lived dangerously: the association of aristocracy and danger and obligation is as congenial to Miss Moore as is the rest of the "flower and fruit of all that noted superiority." Some of her poems have the manners or manner of ladies who learned a little before birth not to mention money, who neither point nor touch, and who scrupulously abstain from the mixed, live vulgarity of life. "You sit still if, whenever you move, something jingles," Pound quotes an officer of the old school as saying. There is the same aristocratic abstention behind the restraint, the sitting still as long as it can, of this poetry. "The passion for setting people right is in itself an afflictive disease. / Distaste which takes no credit to itself is best," she says in an early poem; and says, broadly and fretfully for her, "We are sick of the earth, / sick of the pig-sty, wild geese and wild men." At such moments she is a little disquieting (she speaks for everybody, in the best of the later poems, in a way in which she once could not); one feels like quoting against her her own, "As if a death-mask could replace / Life's faulty excellence," and blurting that life-masks have their disadvantages too. We are uncomfortable—or else too comfortable—in a world in which feeling, affection, charity, are so entirely divorced from sexuality and power, the bonds of the flesh. In this world of the poems there are many thoughts, things, animals, sentiments, moral insights; but money and passion and power, the brute fact that *works,* whether or not correctly, whether or not precisely—the whole Medusa-face of the world: these are gone. In the poem called "Marriage" marriage, with sex, children, and elementary economic existence missing, is an absurd unlikely affair, one that wouldn't fool a child; and, of course, children don't get married. But this reminds me how un-childish, un-young, Miss Moore's poems always are; she is like one of those earlier ages that dressed children as adults, and sent them off to college at the age of eleven—though the poems dress their children in animal-skins, and send them out into the wilderness to live happily ever after. Few poets have as much moral insight as Miss Moore; yet in her poems morality usually *is* simplified into self-abnegation, and Gaugin always seems to stay home with his family—which is right, but wrong in a way, too. Poems which celebrate morality choose more between good and evil, and less between lesser evils and greater goods, than life does, so that in them morality is simpler and more beautiful than it is in life, and we feel our attachment to it strengthened.

"Spine-swine (the edgehog misnamed hedgehog)," echidna, echino-
dern, rhino, the spine pig or porcupine—"everything is battle-dressed";
so the late poem named "His Shield" begins. But by then Miss Moore
has learned to put no trust in armour, says, "Pig-fur won't do, I'll wrap /
myself in salamander-skin like Presbyter John," the "inextinguishable
salamander" who "revealed / a formula safer than / an armourer's:
the power of relinquishing / what one would keep," and whose
"shield was his humility." And "What Are Years" begins "All are
naked, none are safe," and speaks of overcoming our circumstances by
accepting them; just as "Nevertheless" talks not about armour, not
about weapons, but about what is behind or above them both: "The
weak overcomes its / menace, the strong over- / comes itself. What is
there / like fortitude? What sap / went through that little thread / to
make the cherry red!" All this is a wonderfully appealing, a disarming
triumph; yet not so appealing, so disarming, so amused and imaginative and doubtful and tender, as her last look at armour, the last poem
of her *Collected Poems*. It is called "Armour's Undermining Modesty";
I don't entirely understand it, but what I understand I love, and
what I don't understand I love almost better. I will quote most of
the last part of it:

> No wonder we hate poetry,
> and stars and harps and the new moon. If tributes cannot
> be implicit,
>
>> give me diatribes and the fragrance of iodine,
>> the cork oak acorn grown in Spain;
>> the pale-ale-eyed impersonal look
>> which the sales-placard gives the bock beer buck.
> What is more precise than precision? Illusion.
> Knights we've known,
>
>> like those familiar
>> now unfamiliar knights who sought the Grail . . .
>
>> . . . did not let self bar
>> their usefulness to others who were
>> different. Though Mars is excessive
>> in being preventive,
> heroes need not write an ordinall of attributes to
> enumerate what they hate.
>
>> I should, I confess,
>> like to have a talk with one of them about excess,
>> and armour's undermining modesty
>> instead of innocent depravity.
> A mirror-of-steel uninsistence should countenance
> continence,

objectified and not by chance,
there in its frame of circumstance
of innocence and altitude
in an unhackneyed solitude.
There is the tarnish; and there, the imperishable wish.

Likings of an Observationist

by Kenneth Burke

This book is splendid. My enthusiasm is due not just to the great satisfaction I find in reading it, but also to the fact that it can be used. I can think of no book better able to make clear the kind of scruples that can be involved in the writing of a sentence. If *Predilections* doesn't quickly become required reading for students of college English throughout the country, then the fault lies with our English departments.

Miss Moore is so inveterately apt at quotation, one is tempted to review her book similarly, even to the extent of quoting her quoting someone quoting. Her critical "predilections" are the perfect analogue of her poetic "observations." She shifts so naturally between the *liber scriptus* of art and the *liber vivus* of nature, one is never quite sure whether her subject is personal conscience or poetic imagination. She can make us realize the innate rottenness of a person who squanders commas just because they are readily available. Or more specifically, she makes us so alert to the conscientiousness of the comma, in keeping with her view of punctuation as a form of punctuality, that we begin to fear for our own souls, asking ourselves uneasily whether we have erred, too, in these subtly significant matters. And when she quotes in her special way of quoting, we see her carving a text out of a text, much like carving a personal life out of life in general.

Though her book is essentially a record of appreciations, my delight in its usefulness induces me to praise it primarily as an ever wary sequence of admonitions, a study in stylistic scruples. Sometimes, perhaps she is too severe, and she might send a man through sheer despair on the downward path of loose writing, when a bit more leniency might have kept him still striving for improvement. But in general her book should have a wholesome effect as regards the problems of Advanced Remedial Writing, thereby helping us readers, too, with our inborn problems of Advanced Remedial Reading. (I had started to say "a very wholesome effect," but Miss Moore warns us against the use of intensifiers that don't intensify.)

"Likings of an Observationist." Kenneth Burke's review of *Predilections*. From *Poetry*, LXXXVII (January, 1956), 239–47. Copyright 1956 by The Modern Poetry Association. Reprinted by permission of the author and editor of *Poetry*.

Her criticism is done with the kind of generosity that is sure to reward readers, since she is always eager to note, for our delectation, those moments when a writer is at his best. Reading her criticism is like borrowing a book from the personal library of a skilled reader who underlined all the good spots. Even in the case of a bad book, we couldn't be robbed by reading a selection of the brief flashes in which the book may have been good. And we are further protected by the fact that *Predilections* treats of no bad books, the selections dealing with the best in the best of our contemporaries.

Miss Moore's penchant for quotation leads naturally into a love of the succinct (or derives from it). Fittingly, she refers to the aphorism as "one of the kindlier phases of poetic autocracy." And the reprinting of some early remarks on Sir Francis Bacon helps us to see how the cult of the succinct (in either image or idea) can lead, through the love of aphorism, to a particular concern with the maxims of morality, and so to an interest in strategies and tactics generally, as with her citations showing how Bacon's "insight into human idiosyncrasy has a flavor of Machiavelli."

But her very love of precision, in leading her to dot her pages with "porcupine quills," also raises the problem with which she is constantly wrestling. For precision snips things off; its particular good pickiness and choosiness tends to break the continuity. Though she says that the poet writes under the sign of "therefore" (as when she finds in William Carlos Williams "the *ergo* of the medieval dialectician, the 'therefore' which is the distinguishing mark of the artist"), we dare remember that she entitled one of her own volumes *Nevertheless,* while her ways with the quotation mark make for a maximum number of cullings connected by "and" (though with the word itself usually omitted, or supplanted by some transitional remark designed to usher us from one exhibit to the next).

The principle of "nevertheless" doubtless sums up her unchallenging kind of independence. It seems to say, in effect, "Everybody is going that way; nevertheless I will go this way, even to the extent of sometimes going that way." As for the "therefore" (which she can discern beneath Dr. Williams' "chains of incontrovertibly logical apparent non-sequiturs"), in her criticism it rarely if ever has such a sheerly Aristotelian form as we might get were we to say: "The poem has such-and-such a beginning; therefore it has such-and-such a middle; and given its developments up to this point, it therefore has such-and-such an end." Her therefores suggest rather a cogent relationship between the artist as personal center and his art as impersonal circumference, as were one to say: "The center being such-and-such, therefore such-and-such notable radiations are to be found at various points along the circumference." Or, "The poet has such-and-such scruples, therefore he makes such-and-such observations."

Her very aptitude at quotation and her love of condensation incline her to leave unanalyzed whatever aspects of a work do not naturally lend themselves to treatment in terms of aphorism or imaginal miniatures. Perhaps her early essay on Henry James is the weakest in this regard. Though the novel is a form in which the shell is every bit as important as the kernels, here too she expands her main efforts on extracting such kernels as might be the major virtue of a La Rochefoucauld or of her favorite lyric poets. But we miss a concerted concern with the problems of over-all development, of situational involvements, of thematic alignments, of ways in which the dramatis personae (or "novellae personae"?) mesh with one another.

The opening sentences of her piece written in connection with the granting of The Dial Award to William Carlos Williams indicate how well she can infuse an almost pedantic literalness with the moodiness of impressionistic criticism:

> William Carlos Williams is a physician, a resident of New Jersey, the author of prose and verse. He has written of "fences and outhouses built of barrel-staves and parts of boxes," of the "sparkling lady" who "passes quickly to the seclusion of her carriage," of Weehawken, of "The Passaic, that filthy river," of "hawsers that drop and groan," of "a young horse with a green bed-quilt on his withers." His "venomous accuracy," if we may use the words used by him in speaking of the author of *The Raven,* is opposed to makeshifts, self-deceptions and grotesque excuses." Among his meditations are chicory and daisies, Queen Anne's lace, trees—hairy, bent, erect—orchids and magnolias. We need not, as Wallace Stevens has said, "try to . . . evolve a mainland from his leaves, scents and floating bottles and boxes." "What Columbus discovered is nothing to what Williams is looking for." He writes of lions with Ashurbanipal's "shafts bristling in their necks," of "the bare backyard of the old Negro with white hair," of "branches that have lain in a fog which now a wind is blowing away."

Her pages thus become a kind of critic's Mardi Gras, a pageantry of sharply diversified characters momentarily and partially glimpsed as they hurry by. Since the quotation marks escape notice when such writing is read aloud, the page becomes wholly an act of collaboration, a good thing that seems to transcend any one person's ownership, though only someone as expert at this art as she could bring such effects into being.

Similar fine acts of identification mark her chapters on Wallace Stevens ("in each clime the author visits, and under each guise, the dilemma of tested hope confronts him"), T. S. Eliot ("words of special meaning recur with the force of a theme: 'hidden,' 'the pattern,' and 'form' "), E. E. Cummings (his book "a thing of furious nuclear integrities"), Louise Bogan ("Women are not noted for terseness, but Louise Bogan's art is compactness compacted"), W. H. Auden ("stature in diversity"), and the past master of the adapted quotation, Ezra Pound (in whole *Cantos* "The ghost of Homer sings," and whose literary patchwork, making for a special focus upon each individual bit, readily lends itself to her methods).

Jean Cocteau's play, *The Infernal Machine,* is reviewed under the title, "Ichor of Imagination," thereby alluding to a motive suggested by another Cocteau title, *Le Sang d'un Poète.* Perhaps it is typical of her ways that, despite the great critical to-do about the nature of "dramatic irony," she prefers to discuss the subject without mention of the term and as though starting from scratch, thus: "A potent device in fiction or drama is that in which one character describes another to that other, unaware that he addresses the person to whom he speaks."

When she reviews a work by that monumental reader, George Saintsbury, we realize that they have the love of books in common; they compare and contrast most directly at that point where, when she is being minutely painstaking, he must cast darts while hurrying on. But each has a way of trying for a quick succession of characterizations. Other brief items are a review of Georg Brandes' volumes on Goethe (under the suggestively dialectical title, *Besitz und Gemeingut,* combining thoughts of individuality and commonalty), and a three-page review of Sir George Sitwell's book *On the Making of Gardens,* a review that makes us quickly realize how "poetic implacability" can figure in this vocation.

The longer retrospective essay on the 1920–1929 period of *The Dial* might best be characterized by a remark she applies to a book by E. E. Cummings: It is "primarily a compliment to friendship" (though, come to think of it, I guess this formula could fit well with every chapter in this list of "predilections"). It is neatly stepped off, proceeding paragraph by paragraph from topic to topic like the rungs of a ladder: outside, as seen from inside; inside, as seen from outside; notable contributions; personalities; incidents; relations between editors and authors, and so on, through many stages. There is also, at one point, a twitting note, regarding certain *Dial* policies of the earlier years:

> Such titles as *Sense and Insensibility, Engineering With Words, The American Shyness*; and the advertising—especially some lines "Against the Faux Bon" and "technique" in lieu of "genius"—seemed to say, "We like to do this and can do it better than anyone else could"; and I was self-warned to remain remote from so much rightness. . . .

She refers to a "constant atmosphere of excited triumph"—and after a paragraph built about a bit of strongly ideational imagery in a remark of Lawrence, she cites a brief imagery-tinged idea of Yeats. Even the

sheerly business details are listed (for instance, the scrupulous equality
as regards payment to contributors)—and there is the brief wind-up,
ending ". . . I think happily of the days when I was part of it." As
one who himself vividly remembers the more obvious of the things
here observed (but was always woefully lagging as regards her subtler
observations), I find her account so nostalgically appealing that
perhaps I am not qualified to be a judge of it. "Those were days
when, as Robert Herring has said, things were opening out, not
closing in." Yes indeed, except insofar as an opening out might itself
be but the incipient stage of a closing in.[1]

Looking over the list of her personal predilections, we find that
several of them clearly reflect her own salient traits. She is Stevens
fastidious, Eliot conscience-probing, Williams aid-bringing, Pound
citational, Saintsbury book-loving, Bacon aphoristic, Louise Bogan
womanly, Cummings inventive, and a stay-at-home Henry James.
And what of that long essay on which she ends, her tribute to Anna
Pavlova, a high priestess of the dance?

Pavlova seems to have fascinated her as one who represents her
ideals to perfection, though as translated into the terms of a quite
different medium. "To enter the School of the Imperial Ballet," we
are told, "is to enter a convent whence frivolity is banned, and where
merciless discipline reigns." Pavlova's eyes, she says, were "sombered
by solicitude." There is almost a manifesto-like quality in the statement: "in her dancing with persons, remoteness marked her every
attitude." And those who like the trappings of a flimsy mystery might
well ponder this fundamental formula: "She was compelling because
of spiritual force that did not need to be mystery, she so affectionately
informed her technique with poetry." Poetry written under that rule
is bound to be downright. And you can take your choice whether to
call this descriptive vignette a perfect instance of critical predilection
or of poetic observation:

[1] For the record, I might offer this addendum: Miss Moore's generous inclusion
of me in the list of managing editors could be misleading. At various times,
and ranging from weeks to months, I worked as a substitute for members of
the regular staff when on vacation. These jobs went up and down the scale,
in no particular order. And I was paid at the regular rates for all my reviews,
articles, and translations whereas, as Miss Moore rightly says, "Any writing or
translating by the editors was done without payment."

I might also point out, alas, that included in her paragraph of the twitted is
a title of mine, *Engineering With Words*. It concerned what I would now call the
"rhetoric" of Gertrude Stein. If I thereby contrived to terrify Miss Moore somewhat, then I can have the satisfaction of knowing that at least once I repaid her
for the ways in which she, by the gentle mastery of her ways of writing, has
terrified me over and over again. Also, I whisper to myself, she has shown that the
title was at least *material* for a good sentence, as when she says in connection with
the book on gardens: "Engineering zeal in any case is seen to have its verbal
prototype."

It seems to have been an idiosyncrasy of Pavlova's that one hand should copy rather than match the other, as in the Aimé Stevens portrait, in which the hands, holding a string of jade and lifted as though to feel the rain, tend both in the same direction, from left to right (Pavlova's right), instead of diverging equilaterally with the oppositeness of horns. In *Spring Flowers*, the right foot turning left is imitated by the left foot's half-moon curve to the left. *Giselle*—hands reaching forward, feet (tiptoe) in lyrelike verticals—is all of a piece. Everything moves together, like a fish leaping a weir.

So far, we have been considering the pieces that go from the particular to the general. The two opening essays, *Feeling and Precision* and *Humility, Concentration, and Gusto,* proceed rather from the general to the particular. However, the difference between the two kinds is narrowed by the fact that Miss Moore never allows herself the characteristic shortcut of the philosopher or scientist, who may follow along a chain of abstractions. On the contrary, at each step she generalizes only to the extent allowed by the specimen she holds in front of her.

Another word for "feeling" in the first of these two essays (*Feeling and Precision*) is the "inarticulate," while "precision" is correspondingly equated with the "articulate." "Needs" and "emotion" are other synonyms for the "feeling" side; other equivalents for "precision" are "expression," "diction," "exactitude," "accuracy," and "explicitness." Thus, when she says that art "is but an expression of our needs," the two sides of the duality are clear. But when she goes on to say that art "is feeling, modified by the writer's moral and technical insights," the two-term alignment seems to be splitting into a three-term one. For whereas "technical insights" would presumably be on the "precision" side, the "moral" element would seem to be on this side only insofar as it is *insight,* while in other respects I should think that it belonged on the side of "feeling" ("emotion," "needs," the "inarticulate").

Thus, we could say either that the term "moral" in her scheme ambiguously belongs on both sides of the feeling-precision alignment, or that it reveals a tendency of the dyadic system to become triadic. Elsewhere in the book (p. 46) she says: "there is in Wallace Stevens a certain demureness of statement, as when—setting down what he has to say with the neatest kind of precision . . ." etc. In effect this remark equates "precision" with "demureness of statement," whereat we note that the word "demureness," when applied to "statement," also combines the "moral" and the "technical," as in her previously cited expression, "the writer's moral and technical insights."

At first glance, this slight terministic perturbation might look like imprecision, and at the very moment when the talk is of precision. But in a subtler sense it is the fifth essence of precision. For the motivational center of Miss Moore's work, both as poetic observation and as critical predilection, is in the fusion whereby one can never be quite sure whether her judgments are ethical or esthetic.

In any case, whether you think of this two-termed essay as having a further term which partakes ambiguously of both, or as incipiently three-termed, the essay that follows it in the book, and was written four years after the first, is explicitly three-termed. "Three foremost aids which occur to me," she says, "are humility, concentration, and gusto." And near the end of the essay she gives her three terms a pedagogic slant when she sums up: "Humility is an indispensable teacher, enabling concentration to heighten gusto."

It would make for confusion rather than clarification, if we tried to trace exactly how the cuts made by these three terms overlap upon the cuts made by the previous two. It should be enough for our present purposes to note that whereas people generally tend to think of "humility" as a moral virtue, Miss Moore often thinks of it as an intellectual or technical one—or, rather, as the point at which personal character and poetic aptitude meet. It shades into "judicious modesty," which is apparently motivated more by diplomatic considerations than sheer humility would be, yet which she also seems to look upon as genuine in its way.

Perhaps we should mention another three-part set, in one of the essays already mentioned, some pages on Ezra Pound entitled: "Teach, Stir the Mind, Afford Enjoyment." As she points out, the formula, to which she subscribes, is after the analogy of Cicero's three offices of the orator (an alignment also borrowed by St. Augustine in Part IV of his *De Doctrina Christiana,* on Christian rhetoric). But whereas both Cicero and Augustine look upon both teaching and pleasing as but preparatory offices leading to the changing ("moving" or "bending") of people's minds, it is notable that in the version to which Miss Moore subscribes, the second and third offices change places. The rearrangement is presumably in response to the fact that she is adapting to the ends of *poetic appeal* a terminology originally concerned with *rhetorical persuasion.*

Looking at the book from another angle, let us review some of the problems with which Miss Moore is characteristically exercised.

First, there is the problem stemming from the fact that "precision," frankness, uncompromising honesty of statement must coexist with "reserve," "restraint," the effort to keep within the bounds of "our natural reticence."

Closely allied with this search for a mean there is her great predilection for the "art of understatement." Thus she links Wallace Stevens and T. S. Eliot on the basis of their "reticent candor and emphasis by understatement." Elsewhere, she speaks of a "fascination" in "mere understatement." We might say that she writes Under the

Sign of the Figure of Litotes. (A possible minority report here could plead that the classic ideal of *to prepon* should distrust understatement, too, except as an occasional rhetorical device that is most effective when sandwiched in among statements that amplify and statements that are neither over nor under. Miss Moore herself would be the first to recognize that understatement can be supercilious. For she notes that the attempt to be concise, by making one say too little rather than too much, can make writing "seem overcondensed, so that the author is resisted as being enigmatic or disobliging or arrogant.")

Her main concern is with the dignity and responsibility of her calling—a calling in which, by her rules, one avoids the risk of arrogance by imposing upon oneself whatever stylistic commandments one would impose upon others.

Since she is ever on the alert for new ways of saying old things, if we habitually think of A as acting upon B, she will be sure to like the mild stylistic perversity whereby B is presented as acting upon A. Thus, as an example of "precision" in Hopkins she quotes "his saying about some lambs he had seen frolicking in a field, 'It was as though it was the ground that tossed them.' "

She inclines to cull Beatitude-like paradoxes of failure: "He's due to fail if he succeeds" . . . "hope that in being frustrated becomes fortitude" . . . "The right to fail that is worth dying for" . . . "How wrong we are in always being right" . . . "Weakness is power . . . handicap is proficiency . . . the scar is a credential" . . . "an inescapable lesson . . . that discipline results in freedom." Nor should we forget the variant in one of her own poems: "hindered to succeed." However, at one point the idea takes on the appearance of a slightly less Swoboda-like method, when she says: "A critic that would have us 'establish axes of reference by knowing the *best of each kind of written thing*' has persisted to success." And her view of humility as "armor" falls somewhat within this realm.

Her kind of thinking shows up tonally in inclination towards pun-like expressions: art vs. "artificial art"; "reverent, and almost reverend, feeling"; "imagination and the imaginer" as distinct from "images and imagers"; "by heresay—or heresy"; "humility, alas can border on humiliation"; "reverie which was reverence"; "will power has its less noble concomitant, willfulness."

She is for the writer who "goes right on doing what idiosyncrasy tells him to do." She would "ensure naturalness." Typically, she picks from Henry James the maxim: "Don't try to be anyone else." If one but knows how to be overwhelmingly honest, then he can safely and emphatically subscribe to her dictum that "any writer overwhelmingly honest about pleasing himself is almost sure to please others." And it is almost a forgone conclusion that, given such a point of view, she would quote with approval Wallace Stevens' line, "As the man the state, not as the state the man."

There are lots of things still to be noted. But we have covered the ground generally. However, we find one especially superb distinction still left over. What to do with it?

Let's put it last: "William Carlos Williams objects to urbanity—to sleek and natty effects—and this is a good sign if not always a good thing."

"A good sign if not always a good thing." Surely that is perfect precision.

A Few Bricks from Babel

by Howard Nemerov

Offhand I would probably have shared what seems a widespread impression that Marianne Moore was admirably qualified, not only by talent but by sympathy as well, to translate the *Fables* of La Fontaine: this impression appears to have been based on a very rapid summing-up of both poets: "Ah, yes—animals." But there is, I find, a great distance between a Moore jerboa and a La Fontaine rat, and because I enjoy some of Miss Moore's poetry a good deal I am sorry to have to say that the results of this cooperation strike me not as merely inadequate or mediocre but as in a positive way terrible. My fine critical hindsight tells me now, what it didn't warn me of beforehand, that Miss Moore has never been a fabulist at all, that her animals never acted out her moralities; that their function was ever to provide a minutely detailed, finely perceived symbolic knot to be a center for the pattern of her recondite meditations; that what she shares with La Fontaine is a shrewdness and delicacy of the moral judgment, but that the two poets' ways of getting there—their *fables,* in fact—are so different as to be opposed. I still feel, with somewhat less conviction than before, that Miss Moore might have got a happier result by setting herself to *tell* La Fontaine's stories in English, for it seems that a critical factor in the failure of these translations may have been an uncertainty about the ideal degree of her dependence on the French: as poems to be read in English, they are irritatingly awkward, elliptical, complicated, and very jittery as to the meter; as renderings of the French they vacillate between pedantic strictness and strange liberty.

I began with the intention of reading the volume through without reference to the original—since if the poems could not be read as English it did not seem to matter how accurate they might be as translations—but was at once pulled up by the dedication to the Dauphin of which Miss Moore has printed the French on the facing page. Inescapably, "Je chante les héros dont Ésope est le père" had come out as "I sing when Aesop's wand animates my lyre." There is nothing necessarily wrong with this: it is precisely the *unnecessary* distance

From "A Few Bricks from Babel" by Howard Nemerov. From *The Sewanee Review*, LXII (Winter 1954), 655-59. Copyright 1954 by The University of the South, © 1962 by Howard Nemerov. Reprinted by permission of the author.

from the original which is odd. And in the last couplet, where La Fontaine's sentiment is rigorously conventional—"Et, si de t'agréer je n' emporte le prix / J'aurai du moins l'honneur de l'avoir entrepris"— Miss Moore has written something much more friendly: "And if I have failed to give you real delight, / My reward must be that I had hoped I might." I read on according to intention but with an occasional uneasy sense of missing things; and presently began turning to the French simply to make certain here and there of what was being said. For example, in the fable about belling the rat (II,2) the rats hold their meeting while the cat goes courting:

> Now as he climbed, or creeps lengthened his loin
> In his renegade quest for some tabby he'd court,
> Through the witches' sabbath in which they'd consort,
> Surviving rats had seen fit to convene
> In a corner to discuss their lot.

I was struck, or maybe stricken is a better word, by "creeps lengthened his loin." Application to La Fontaine revealed what was behind all this:

> Or un jour qu'au haut et au loin
> Le galant alla chercher femme,
> Pendant tout le sabbat qu'il fit avec sa dame,
> Le demeurant des Rats tint chapitre en un coin
> Sur la nécessité présente.

It is easy to see how *"loin"* became "loin," though not so easy to see why, or what has been gained except a false rime to "convene." But a number of other difficulties come up as a result of this investigation. Granting the necessity of lengthening the first two octosyllabic lines to ten syllables and twelve, is there any other justification for "renegade quest"? Even if the cat has earlier been called "un diable," why should the sabbath be a "witches' sabbath," when the meaning is simply that the rats got a rest? Why confuse the issue with "they," which grammatically seems to want to mean the rats (since "consort" doesn't have to have a sexual meaning)? And why, having expanded the mere suggestion of "au haut et au loin" to the monstrous "as he climbed, or creeps lengthened his loin," does Miss Moore then economize by cutting out La Fontaine's thematic figure—whereby in the moral the rats become "chapitres de moines . . . chapitres de chanoines"—and give us "had seen fit to convene" for "tint chapitre en un coin"? So that she can go on to translate "doyen" once as "doyen" and then later on as "dean"?

Perhaps these are quibbles; I'm sorry if so. And I would give them up instantly if it seemed that the sacrifice of simplicity, accuracy and sense had resulted in some clear gain in the English version; but it was the oddity of the English which in the first place drew my notice. And while the first line of that passage is outstandingly and exceptionally silly, the general nature of the faults it indicates can be illustrated by numerous examples, of which I shall give a few.

Miss Moore habitually invents metaphors for her poet. La Fontaine talks of people pretending to sophistication and travel, who, "caquetants au plus dru, / Parlent de tout, et n'ont rien vu," for which Miss Moore supplies, "Boasting he's seen this spot and that, / Whereas his alps have all been flat." Gratuitous, probably harmless in this instance, but at least irrelevant and probably destructive when "Les petites, en toute affaire, / Esquivent fort aisément" becomes "modesty anywhere, / Glides in as when silk is sewn." Even when the figure itself is clever, particularly when it is clever, it is disturbing to feel the immediate suspicion that La Fontaine wrote something different.

Miss Moore tends to extremes of latinity, sometimes I suspect because she will do anything for a rime, often a false rime. If a falcon says to a capon, "Ton peu d'entendement / Me rend tout étonné," Miss Moore writes, "Wretched phenomenon / Of limitation. Dullard, what do you know?" La Fontaine begins to consider the head and tail of the serpent with: "Le serpent a deux parties / Du genre humaine ennemies," and Miss Moore brings out, "A serpent has mobility / Which can shatter intrepidity."

The general objection, of which the two foregoing objections are specific instances, is that Miss Moore is so often found going the long way around, making complexities out of simplicities, loading lines with detail until they are corrupted in sense or measure, and writing, in consequence, absurdly bad English. "Une Huitre, que le flot y venoit d'apporter" (to the beach, that is) appears in translation as "an oyster amid what rollers scatter."

It is not much of a compliment to say that there are better things in this translation than these examples suggest; there would have to be. But I give the examples because they seem to me to typify the faults in Miss Moore's practice. Even when things are going well so far as the translation is concerned, the tone and texture of the language remain very uncertain; just as we think we begin to hear in English the modesty and humorous dignity of the fabulist, along comes some monstrous circumlocution or complicated syntactical maneuver to ensure the fall of the rime. And meanwhile the meter is, to say the least of it, very strange; it is syllabic, I think, and Miss Moore in her Foreword mentions "my effort to approximate the original rhythms of the Fables," but what emerges in English is frequently a kind of gallop now and again flattened by a reduction to prose. The following passage seems a fair sample:

> Then he burned bones when they found a roadstead,
> Soiling Jove's nostrils with the noisomeness engendered,

And said, "There, Sire; accept the homage I've tendered—
Ox perfume to be savored by almighty Jupiter.
These fumes discharge my debt; I am from now on a free man."

I am sorry to be unable to like these translations better than I do; the labor of their preparation must have been long and hard, and the quality of Miss Moore's original talent justified very high expectations. The difficulties of the matter seem to have faced up to, but rather added to than overcome by the translator's own predilections and powers. One final quotation will perhaps serve as a summary of what appears to me to have gone wrong, as a suggestion, too, that somewhere near a poem of La Fontaine there exists, potentially, a poem of Marianne Moore, but that the two have not come into phase. The Epilogue of Book Six begins thus:

> Bornons ici cette carrière:
> Les longs ouvrages me font peur.
> Loin d'épuiser une matière,
> On n'en doit prendre que la fleur.

> Our peregrination must end there.
> One's skin creeps when poets persevere.
> Don't press pith from core to perimeter;
> Take the flower of the subject, the thing that is rare.

This passage was translated by Elizur Wright in 1841 as follows:

> Here check we our career.
> Long books I greatly fear.
> I would not quite exhaust my stuff;
> The flower of subjects is enough.

The general question raised by this comparison is as much concerned with what translators try to do as with what they actually get done; whatever we think of Elizur Wright's version—I hold it to be very fine—we must agree that it shows a detailed deference to the meaning of the original *and* an idea, perhaps a very simple idea, of what English verse is. Now the famous revolution in modern poetry, accompanied by a special uprising in the translation business, destroyed at least the security of that idea of English verse if not the idea itself; but this revolution, product of a few great talents, itself produced no idea of English verse but only the examples of the few great talents, with the stern recommendation: Go thou and do otherwise. It did produce some general notions, what Mr. Pound called his "results," and Miss Moore declares that "the practice of Ezra Pound has been for me a governing principle," but it is doubtful that these general notions, in so complex an affair as translation, ever did more than prescribe avoidances; and a principle cannot substitute for a habit of mind and ear, nor for ease and fluency in the measure or the idiom.

I have observed, too, that modern translations are praised precisely because they are modern translations. Since Mr. Eliot's celebrated re-mark about Gilbert Murray all those scholarly gentlemen who "did" (often indeed in both senses) "the classics" have been held mightily in disrepute, while recent translators are flattered by critics and publishers (and sometimes preen themselves prefatorily) on writing their versions in "modern, idiomatic English," "the speech of living English, the lan-guage a poet would choose for his own work today." But this sort of judgment seems to put an undue strain on the qualities of "living English," and one thinks mournfully of the ghosts of Golding, Chap-man, Pope, who never had a chance.

For the translator's problem, a special and poignant case of the artistic problem generally, is that of making flat maps of a round world; some distortion is inevitable. Bearings and distances become accurate at the expense of sizes and shapes, and the end result will never *look* much like the real thing but the hope is that real navigation will be possible with its aid.

Supreme in Her Abnormality

by Hugh Kenner

The achievement of Marianne Moore's version of La Fontaine is to have brought over a number of the 241 poems virtually intact, and (by dint of persevering with the least tractable) to have discovered the principles of a badly needed idiom, urbane without slickness and brisk without imprecision. Since Chaucer's fell into disuse, English verse, constantly allured by the sonorous and catachrestic, hasn't had a reliable *natural* idiom that can imitate the speech of civilized men and still handle deftly subjects more complex than the ones whose emotions pertain, like Wordsworth's, to hypnotic obviousness; hence nothing existed for a La Fontaine to be translated into. Pope's ease (as distinguished from his wit) is slippery, treacherous even in his own hands; Dryden's directness clangs on iron stilts; and the "naturalness" of various minor eighteenth-century compoundings—tinctured by ballads and diluted by preoccupations with nerveless diction—offers no equivalent at all for La Fontaine's hard neatness. Miss Moore's best work demonstrates that a specialization of one language may be the best possible parallel for the simplicities of another; the very artless with which she can employ a Latinate diction without sounding as though she had read Vergil ("Clemency may be our best resource" for *"Plus fait douceur que violence"*) helps to keep her least natural locutions in touch with speech.

Her artlessness isn't at all like La Fontaine's transparency; it resembles the "unconscious fastidiousness" which she once illustrated by adducing "childish . . . determination to make a pup eat his meat from the plate." [1] Her air of plunging without premeditation into tortuousness which she subdues *ambulando* is sometimes annoying, but it confers virtue too, complicating the plain sense enough to fend off *simplesse*. La Fontaine's curiously *pastoral* urbanity (not the least like Pope's), his devaluing of lions and busy kings, his citation of self-sufficient foxes or asses wise too late, and his implicit appeal to the wisdom of a Greek slave who perceived a wealth of analogies between

[1] "Critics and Connoisseurs," in Marianne Moore's *Collected Poems*.

the courtly world and the animal kingdom because he stood outside
both of them, present the translator with problems perhaps greater
than those posed by his intricate rhythms and rhymes. Previous
translators, assuming that the transparent sense will look after itself,
have been misled into foisting on their author a world of simple
follies from which one can detach oneself by an act as facile as
walking out of the zoo, in order to live by a few *simpliste* maxims.
His situations are postulated with misleading ease:

> Maître corbeau, sur un arbre perché,
>   Tenait en son bec un fromage;
> Maître renard, par l'odeur alléché,
>   Lui tint à peu près ce langage:

A crow with some cheese, and a fox attracted by the smell; nothing
more casual (assuming that foxes like cheese). The fox has a few conventional phrases:

> "Hé bonjour, Monsieur du Corbeau.
> Que vous êtes joli! que vous me semblez beau!
>   Sans mentir, si votre ramage
>   Se rapporte à votre plumage,
> Vous êtes le phénix des hôtes de ces bois."

Perceiving, however, that the French neatness would make for empty
English, Miss Moore with incomparable deftness complicates the
diction very considerably:

> On his airy perch among the branches
>   Master Crow was holding cheese in his beak.
> Master Fox, whose pose suggested fragrances,
>   Said in language which of course I cannot speak,
>   "Aha, superb Sir Ebony, well met.
> How black! who else boasts your metallic jet!
>   If your warbling were unique,
>   Rest assured, as you are sleek,
> One would say that our wood had hatched nightingales."

The "airy perch," the pose suggesting fragrances, "Sir Ebony," the
"metallic jet," the "warbling," the sleekness and the nightingales we
owe to Miss Moore; La Fontaine by contrast sketches his situation
with a few swift platitudes. What has happened, however, is not
simply the interposition of a more crinkly language; the tone, and so
our relationship to the fable, is newly complicated. *"A peu près ce
langage"* is one of La Fontaine's negligent gestures of paraphrase; he
wasn't there at the time (as he frequently tells us in other fables), but
feels it safe from general knowledge of flatterers to assume that the

sense was about as follows. Miss Moore's deliciously practical "language which of course I cannot speak" effects at a stroke, however, the complete separation of this incident from its human analogies: this is fox- and crow-talk. Hence the "Sir Ebony," the "metallic jet" and the rest of the specificities; hence too the pervading *strangeness* of idiom, which she isn't at all at pains to mitigate. In the authoress of "The Jerboa" and "The Pangolin" this strangeness may be idiosyncrasy, but here idiosyncrasy is as good as principle.[2] La Fontaine's crow, responding to the fox's flattery, *"pour montrer sa belle voix, ouvre un large bec."* He reminds us of a man. But in Miss Moore's version,

> All aglow, Master Crow tried to run a few scales,
> > Risking trills and intervals,
> Dropping the prize as his huge beak sang false.

Exquisitely absurd, because he is unambiguously a crow; and his corvine ungainliness gives the twentieth-century fable an edge the seventeenth-century ones acquire, in a different language, by different and more insinuating means.

That a Marianne Moore crow even in a translation should be unmistakably a crow, not a symbol, is what we should expect from the use to which she puts the celebrated animals in her poems. Her characteristic beast is the only thing of its kind prized for its uniqueness ("an aye-aye is not / an angwan-tíbo, potto, or loris"[3]); her "zebras, supreme in their abnormality," and "elephants with their fog-coloured skin" don't impress us as members of the animal kingdom but as grotesque individualities; while the indubitably human cat in the same poem[4] who speaks the astringent moral isn't "people" but a well-remembered person. When she uses an elephant to voice her characteristic theme in "Melancthon":

> Openly, yes,
> with the naturalness
> > of the hippopotamus or the alligator
> > > when it climbs out on the bank to experience the
>
> sun, I do these
> things which I do, which please
> > no one but myself. . . .

it isn't the elephant's abstract ponderosity that recommends it to her as a persona: rather, the gesture it performs by existing at all

---

[2] Mr. Eliot made the fundamental observation about her diction in 1923 . . . [See T. S. Eliot's "Marianne Moore (1923)" above pp. 48–51.]

[3] "Four Quartz Crystal Clocks."

[4] "The Monkeys."

> (for the
> patina of circumstance can but enrich what was
> there to begin with)

allies itself with her own temperamental taut self-sufficiency, mutating primness into resilience.

The uncompromising inhabitants of Miss Moore's zoo, cross-bred with the citizens of the urbane La Fontaine's hierarchic animal kingdom, lend to an enterprise endangered by obviousness a jaunty manner of speaking that always arrests and often wholly entrances the modern reader:

> A mite of a rat was mocking an elephant
> As it moved slowly by, majestically aslant,
>   Valued from antiquity,
>   Towering in draped solemnity
>   While bearing along in majesty
>   A queen of the Levant—
>   With her dog, her cat, and sycophant,
> Her parakeet, monkey, anything she might want—
> On their way to relics they wished to see. . . .

Every word has its presence, and the tone is inimitable. Some of the beginnings (less often the endings) are less happy:

> When warm spring winds make the grass green
> And animals break from winter captivity,
> A certain wolf, like other creatures grown lean,
>   Was looking about for what food there might be.
> As said, a wolf, after a winter that had been hard
> Came on a horse turned out to grass. . . .

This isn't the way to begin this story, though it is a desperate attempt to include all the words that are in the French. La Fontaine, however, arranges them differently; he begins with the wolf (*"Un certain loup dans la saison / Que les tièdes zéphyrs ont l'herbe rajeunie. . . ."*) and the *"Un loup, dis-je"* five lines later is accompanied by a discreet cough as he realizes that he has been drawn into digressive poetizing about the spring. Miss Moore, on the other hand, began with the spring, then got around to the wolf, and looks excessively awkward when two lines later she has to pretend that she is remembering with a start a subject only just introduced. Given her opening, omission of the "As said, a wolf" clause would make infinitely better sense; it is probably a sound rule in translating to omit what won't function in your new poem. Whether her native stubbornness interfered, or a failure to comprehend La Fontaine's delicate gesture involved itself with a determination to render his faults word for word as well as his beauties, there is no guessing. There is a third possibility. From an exceedingly odd foreword to the volume we learn of a condition—presumably the publishers'—"that Professor Harry Levin examine the work to ensure a sound equivalent to the French";[5] further that after Mr. Levin's "scholastic intensities of supervision" Mr. Monroe Engel of the Viking Press "ameliorated . . . persisting ungainlinesses"; finally that "as consulting editor at the Press Malcolm Cowley pronounced certain portions of the text 'rather far from the French'; he has contributed lines in addition to pedagogy." With such a committee at work, one may trust that every word of the French has gotten represented somewhere; it is perhaps surprising that Miss Moore was able to get away with inserting "Aha, superb Sir Ebony."

It is only her habitual nonchalance that prompts inquiry into Miss Moore's poetic lapses; their magnitude is seldom sufficient to damage even single poems, and the enterprise as a whole succeeds astonishingly. As often as not they occur where oddness of expression (for the sake of tone) complicates the sense beyond easy decipherment:

> Where in spring find the flowers gardens bore,
> Like Flora's own in bloom at his door?

seems an unnecessarily tortuous way of saying that Flora's choicest gifts grew in this man's garden. When Miss Moore gets preoccupied (understandably) with tucking all the words into the given rhythms and rhyme schemes she frequently produces what may be the neatest solution to this particular crossword puzzle, but is not the best way of conveying the subject at hand in English.

It is often, however, the best way of creating a climate of mind, not heretofore available in English, in which the wit of the Fables can thrive. All convincing translation remains miraculous, but the normal excellence of this one is surprisingly sustained: the work of a deliberate and indefatigable intelligence, which earns its reward when the translator's special diction, personal and by existing literary standards impure, re-creates the French aplomb with an absoluteness no careful reader is going to ascribe to luck. The fable, already cited, about the rat mocking the elephant illustrates this order of triumph as well as any.

---

[5] Though no one's vigilance prevented *"Le fantôme brillant attire une alouette"* from getting rendered by ". . . allured by his bright mirroring *of her* a lark" (p. 131). Surely it was the sun's reflection, not her own, that attracted her?

Prosody and Tone:
The "Mathematics" of Marianne Moore

by Robert Beloof

Critics seldom mention, and almost never systematically discuss, a poet's prosody (what, after all, is to be gained by facing the fact that for some reason Yeats minded his length of line, the regularity of his stanza, like the meanest newspaper versifier?). Yet certain few poets almost from the first attract especial notice to their prosody, though the comments on them seem often to be half-truths, hallowed by usage, or perceptions whose cause is ill-traced.

Those who have read some of the comments on Marianne Moore's poetry will recall a constant mention of her syllabic prosody (line length determined by count of syllables). Critics are likely to speak of the tautness of her form, the precision of her sensibility. The word "mathematic" has even been used by Randall Jarrell in "The Humble Animal," *Kenyon Review,* April 1953. While one certainly agrees that this gives an accurate sense of that ineffable quality *tone,* one is aware that in fact the true relation between prosody and the tone has not been adequately explored.

What then is the real gestalt of Miss Moore's formal structures? I hope to show that in all but Miss Moore's later poems, the syllabic prosody and attendant devices are so used as to minimize the usual rhythmic possibilities of the syllabic structure, in order to give an effect more nearly approximating free verse, and that as a consequence we must presume the mathematic tone of her poetry is derived from other aspects of her total poetic. I hope to show too that at least a certain number of the later poems, still syllabic, represent a departure from this minimization of the usual syllabic effect, while paradoxically developing a tone in which the sense of dry precision is a less important constituent.

We have indicated that it is a commonplace to speak of Marianne Moore's meter as being syllabic. Actually in the beginning Miss Moore

"Prosody and Tone: The 'Mathematics' of Marianne Moore" by Robert Beloof. From *The Kenyon Review,* XX, No. I (Winter 1958), 116–23. Copyright © 1958 by *The Kenyon Review.* Reprinted by permission of the author and *The Kenyon Review.*

wrote in two formal traditions, the syllabic and the free verse, and, as we shall see, a modified technique is emerging in her later writing.

In selecting her *Collected Poems* (1951), Miss Moore retained 45 poems from the earlier *Selected Poems* (1935). Of those still-approved poems from her work of 20 years ago, 13 are free verse poems. These are: "When I Buy Pictures"; "A Grave"; "The Labours of Hercules"; "New York"; "Snakes, Mongooses, Snake-Charmers and the Like"; "People's Surroundings"; "Bowls"; "Novices"; "Marriage"; "An Octopus"; "Sea Unicorns and Land Unicorns"; "The Monkey Puzzle"; "Silence." A characteristic of all these poems is that they do not attempt to direct the reader's voice through typographic guides, a practice quite common in certain of our contemporary writers of free verse: Pound, Eliot, Cummings, and others. The lines march down the page with no other dramatic aid than the break of each line, and the normal punctuation. Certain of them, particularly "Marriage," are written in a short terse line. Others are written in long lines. The lines in "Snakes, Mongooses, Snake-Charmers and the Like" vary between 12 and 23 syllables. But most of these free verse poems may be said to intermix line lengths.

This intermixture of line lengths is typical also of Miss Moore's syllabic verse. Only two poems have line lengths of the same syllabic count, and to find variations of less than 5 syllables is not at all common. Sometimes the contrast is very marked. In "These Various Scalpels," for instance, a line of one syllable is followed in each stanza by a line of 18 syllables. In general, the poems of closely similar line lengths occur among the later poems. Another distinction between the latest syllabic poems and the earlier ones, is that in the earlier ones almost invariably a firm norm for the syllabic count of a given line is set up over several stanzas, so that though one line in one stanza may vary slightly, the reader has no difficulty in deciding on the normal syllable count. This is not true in some of the later poems (notably "A Face," "The Icosasphere," "Veracities and Verities," "Armour's Undermining Modesty"), where in some lines a norm is never established, though the variance is seldom more than a syllable or two.

In the beginning, then, we find both syllabic and free verse poems. The free verse poems may have a long line or a short line or have an intermixture. Such an intermixture of line lengths is usual in the syllabic poems, here sometimes achieving an extreme variance. Free verse poems stop appearing, and we note some change in the syllabic technique in the later poems. Whereas there was from the first an occasional variation in a given line length, lately she begins to allow herself the liberty of not establishing a precise norm for certain lines, while at the same time the extreme variance of line length tends to lessen.

There are certain matters closely related to metering which should probably be investigated at this point. Rhyme, for instance, appears only sporadically and informally in her free verse poems, but is handled in quite a distinctive way in the syllabic poems. It is usual in the English tradition for a poem to be rhymed or unrhymed, or, where thorn lines exist in a poem with rhyme, to subordinate them numerically to the rhymed lines. Miss Moore is, I venture to say, unique among important poets in her subordination of the rhymed line to the thorn line. In "The Hero" for instance, there are three stanzas, nine lines to a stanza. Only the first and ninth lines of each stanza rhyme, all with the same phonetic unit. In fact, were it not that all the rhymes were the same (go, grow, hero, fro, etc.) the rhyme would be almost totally lost. As it is, its main effect is not intra-stanzaic, as with most rhymes, but inter-stanzaic. Again, however, we notice some alteration of technique in her later poems. There is a gradual numerical increase in rhyme till in some, notably "The Wood Weasel," "A Face," "By Disposition of Angels," "His Shield" and "Armour's Undermining Modesty," it becomes omnipresent. The fact that Miss Moore uses slant rhyme as a variant has been commented upon, but I think it has not been noticed that her slant rhymes are often more emphatic than her true rhymes.

> to the fighting—it's a promise—'We'll
> never hate black, white, red, yellow, Jew,
> Gentile, Untouchable.' We are
> not competent to
> make our vows.

Thus in this passage from "In Distrust of Merits" the solid rhyme "Jew-to" is without question more demure than a slant rhyme like "blood-food," largely because one of the words in the true rhyme set is unimportant grammatically. In fact, since it is the first half of the infinitive, we are forced to move over it. Another method Miss Moore has of moving us quickly over the rhyme is the rhyme achieved by a fracturing of the word as in this example from "Virginia Britannica":

> unscent-
> ed, provident-
> ly hot

If one is *looking* at the poem there is no doubt the unusual visual aspect attracts attention to the rhyme. But if one is *listening* to the poem there is also no question that the rhyme is minimized and approaches nearer to the slight effect of a sound echo within a line.

Thus we can say that, with the exception of some of her later poems, the number of rhymed lines is inferior to the number of thorn lines. She further subdues the solidity of rhyme by mixing slant rhymes in, and sometimes by forcing the reader, by means we have discussed, to give less than the usual emphasis to true rhymes.

These devices, ending a line with a fraction of a word, and ending a line on an article, conjunction or other unimportant part of speech, are used in her syllabic poetry when no question of rhyme is involved. They create, prosodically speaking, the greatest tonal difference to be found between her free verse and her syllabic poetry. For they are almost never discovered in her free verse poems, where the line is based on the sense of phrase, whether of grammar or of breath, and almost always ends with the end of a phrase, or on a noun, verb, or other important part of speech.

As to the effect of her prosody on tone, it is rather clear that Miss Moore has used her syllabic technique to minimize the sense of metric regularity. The sparseness of rhyme sets, the redoubling of the sense of run-on line by ending lines with unimportant words or hyphenations, the leaping between somewhat extreme lengths of line— these are all devices to minimize a firm sense of line as a rhythmic unit. The basic rhythmic power and beauty exploited by syllabic poetry lies traditionally in this firm sense of length of line which becomes a rhythmic unit used contrapuntally against the rhythm of the phrase. She uses this contrapuntal technique to a degree, but it is minimized. Her manipulation of syllabic prosody makes a somewhat unique contribution to the historic use of this form in the devices by which, as we have described, she accomplishes this minimization. Her syllabic prosody, in short, is made to *sound* very much like her free verse poems, and the mathematic tone arises largely from a variety of devices that lie outside the units of measurement—the carefully noted quotes, the very proper precise placing of the word, so often an abstraction, the biological text-like descriptions—from the total habits of a female of exquisite if rather private taste, who domesticates with a tidy assurance; from all these things, surely, but also from the rhythm.

The sparseness of rhyme, the subduing of what rhyme is used, the variety of line lengths, all these devices for heightening the sense of run-on line at the expense of the line as rhythmic unit, are accompanied by an accentual rhythm which is far removed from the subtly varied rise and fall of a poem in a fairly close regular foot. A scansion of part of the poem "The Fish" will reveal the irregularities involved.

Stanza

	I		II
Line 1	I	Line 1	I
Line 2	XXII	Line 2	IXI
Line 3	XXIIIXIII	Line 3	XIXXXXIXI

Line 4   XIXXXII   Line 4   XXIIXI
Line 5   IXXXIXXIX   Line 5   IXXXIIXX

It is clear that, granted the prosody is based on a count of syllables rather than a count of feet, there is still no accentual rhythmic pattern which is developed with anything like enough firmness to establish itself in a pathetic way. Rather, the lack of rhythmic pattern is the basis of its emotional nature.

I have a number of times made certain exceptions with regard to some of her later poems. I mentioned, for instance, that the variation in length of line tends to lessen, that for certain lines it becomes impossible to say what the "right" or "normal" syllable count is, though the range of variation is no more than a syllable or two. I have mentioned that her output of free verse poems ceases, and that in these later syllabic poems rhyme becomes much more frequent and important, and, in certain poems, dominant. Furthermore, one finds that she almost completely stops the practice of fracturing words at line-end. These changes are certainly not insignificant, and have their effect on the tone, which is one of greater formality of statement, together with a more intense passion. But of greater importance than these is the change in accentual rhythm, and an intensification of sound patterns which accompanies that change. Let us scan the first stanza of "In Distrust of Merits":

IXXI IXXI X
IXX *XI XI XI*
     XI XI XI XXI
     I *XI XI*
XI XI XXXIXX
     XI XI XI II *XI*
     III *XI* XX
     IX IX III
     XXIXIXX
     IX IX II

I have italicized here some of the repeated rhythmic themes, and a comparison with the scansion of two stanzas of "The Fish" given above will show that "In Distrust of Merits" has taken on a relatively iambic cast, with free substitution of other rhythmic themes, some of which are in turn repeated.

In her earlier poems Miss Moore is careful to keep the various sound echoes muted. This is tonally in keeping with all the other means we have noted for achieving the tone of carefully rendered didacticism. In the later poems, however, she uses a richer content of sound relationships. Consider the poem, "His Shield." In Stanza I, ll. 1, 2, we have

> The pin-swin or spine-swine
>> (the edgehog miscalled hedgehog) with all his edges
>> out. . . .

and in Stanza 5, ll. 2, 3

> What one would keep; that is freedom. Become
>> dinosaur-
>> skulled, quilled or salamander-wooled, more ironshod.

Or in the poem, "Armour's Undermining Modesty," Stanza 4;

>> give me diatribes and the fragrance of iodine,
>> the cork oak acorn grown in Spain;
>> the pale-ale-eyed impersonal look
>> which the sales-placard gives the bock beer buck.
> What is more precise than precision? Illusion.
> Knights we've known. . . .

The heightened, more lyrical voice of Miss Moore's later poetry is lifted on a combination of a more musical rhythm, and the more intricately wrought pattern of sound which is so apparent in these selections. Peculiarly enough it is in the early poems of Marianne Moore, where the "mathematic" tone is most obvious, that she employs so successfully so many means for reducing the importance of her syllabically determined line. The tone there rises, both in the syllabic and in the free verse poems, from uses of diction and rhythm already discussed. It is in the later poems where (though they are without doubt no less precise) the tone desired is not so much one of precise distinctions, nice contrasts, and slight if portentous ironic gestures—it is here that the particular formal qualities of syllabic poetry are heightened by rhythm and euphony to a tone which is paradoxically not happiest in the drawing room, yet more clearly something of "hammered gold and gold enamelling."

Marianne Moore

by Roy Harvey Pearce

The great hazard of so much of twentieth-century American poetry in the egocentric mode lies, as has been abundantly evident, in its own peculiar *hubris*. Once the poet has committed himself to himself, and to no one else, he runs the risk of poetry for the poet's sake; he runs the risk of having to deny that there is any world of genuine worth except the one he can create. There is thus even in the best of Williams, Aiken, and Cummings, a certain chest-pounding bravado which might well conceal a fear of the unknown and unknowable. They so often tend to overreact, to protest much too loudly. Modesty is not one of their virtues; nor, at their best, need it be. Yet, at their worst, we so often wish that it were. Wit, irony, perspective, a sense of *noblesse oblige* and high-civility, a certain relaxed ease, an easing-up on the reins: all this their way of poetry will not let them have. All this Marianne Moore does have. But she pays a certain cost too: at her worst, she is fussy, gossipy, uncertain as to direction and development. Yet at her best she has a sense of propriety which we can only prize.

She too has a poem, an early one, dealing—and quite explicitly—with the Adamic predicament:

In the Days of Prismatic Colour

not in the days of Adam and Eve, but when Adam
   was alone; when there was no smoke and colour was
fine, not with the refinement
   of early civilization art, but because
   of its originality. . . .

And she goes on to define the clarity of the Adamically-perceived original and the danger of too insistent sophistication and complexity, until:

> In the short-legged, fit-
> ful advance, the gurgling and the minutiae—we have
> the classic
>
> multitude of feet. To what purpose! Truth is no Apollo
> Belvedere, no formal thing. The wave may go over it if
> it likes.
> Know that it will be there when it says,
> "I shall be there when the wave has gone by."

She wants above all to keep her eye on the object, to avoid making it a formal thing. Here she is one with her fellows. But she is more "personal" than they. She catches herself in the act of trying to achieve their sort of heroic, even cosmic, insight; and she pulls back, always to the object. She will not let the thing in itself, of which William Carlos Williams has so much to say, lead to much more than itself. She orders the world of her poems so as to make it yield such insight; but the insights are as modest as the world which is thus ordered. She preaches, especially in her later poems, true enough. But when she does so, she is frank to write like a preacher, for whom the things of this world are, for the time, just not enough. She is not at her best as a preacher—although, as we shall see, her preaching appears to be an inevitable development of her notion of what poems are and what they do. At her best she is the poet of the local, controlled analogy. It is her superb sense of locality and her remarkable control which let her keep the analogy firmly in hand. As poet, she constantly evokes the sort of world Adamic poets must come home to—if only to leave home once more. Her world is the sort from which they begin and from which they so readily wander—getting themselves lost, as they flee from manunkind and his terribly limiting rituals of self-definition.

Her friend Williams, in his accustomed role of prophet become public relations man, wrote of her in 1931:

> The "useful result" [of Miss Moore's poetry] is an accuracy to which [the] simplicity of design greatly adds. The effect is for the effect to remain "true"; nothing loses its identity because of the composition, but the parts in their assembly remain quite as "natural" as before they were gathered. There is no "sentiment"; the softening effect of word upon word is nil; everything is in the style. . . . The general effect is of a rise through the humanities, the sciences, without evading "thought," through anything (if not everything) of the best of modern life; taking whatever there is as it comes, using it and leaving it drained of its pleasure, but otherwise undamaged.

In 1935, introducing her *Selected Poems*, Eliot (by now a prophet turned editor) wrote:

Miss Moore's poetry, or most of it, might be classified as "descriptive" rather than "lyrical" or "dramatic." Descriptive poetry is supposed to be dated to a period, and to be condemned thereby; but it is really one of the permanent modes of expression. In the eighteenth century—or say a period which includes *Cooper's Hill, Windsor Forest,* and *Gray's Elegy* —the scene described is a point of departure for meditations on one thing or another.

Thus two views of the world of Miss Moore's poems: as a series of assemblages of not ideas but things in themselves; and as the scene, and the occasion too, for a series of meditations. I quote these attempts to place Miss Moore's poems in the Adamic and the mythic purviews, because I think they are both quite justified, though not equally, by the nature of those poems. The poems, especially those in the *Selected Poems,* are so cautious and cautionary, so essentially uncommitted, that they may well seem to be characteristic of either of the two major modes of twentieth-century American poetry as I have been attempting to define and elucidate them. But in the four volumes after that—*What Are Years* (1941), *Nevertheless* (1944), and *Like a Bulwark* (1957), and *O To Be a Dragon* (1959)—the case is quite different. Here there are meditations in which a sense of a place or an occasion is made to yield a meaning. Since in such poems the making-yielding formulation is crucial, Miss Moore is here Williams' poet and not Eliot's. She is, with due deliberation, characteristically American. Her later preachments—brilliant exercises in rhetoric which do not quite have the created self-sufficiency of her best poems—have been preachments about the noble and tragic sufficiency of the self. In some of these latter poems it is as though, as an afterthought, she were writing the prolegomenon to her poetry. Poetry, as she wrote in the most celebrated of her earlier poems, is quite bothersome:

Poetry

> I, too, dislike it: there are things that are important beyond
>   all this fiddle.
>   Reading it, however, with a perfect contempt for it, one
>   discovers in
> it, after all, a place for the genuine.

The "genuine"—defined so memorably as "imaginary gardens with real toads in them"—has always been her main concern. For her poetry is a means of identifying the genuine; poetry is where one starts out from, and no more. There is a certain fussy modesty about all this;

and it is pleasing to hear it from her more than once. I think of other such early (i.e., pre-1935) poems as:

> Literature is a phase of life. If
>> one is afraid of it, the situation is irremediable; if
> one approaches it familiarly
>> what one says of it is worthless. Words are constructive
> when they are true; the opaque allusion—the simulated
>> flight
>
> upward—accomplishes nothing.
>
> ("Picking and Choosing")

and:

When I Buy Pictures

> or what is closer to the truth,
> when I look at that of which I may regard myself as the
>> imaginary possessor,
> I fix upon what would give me pleasure in my average
>> moments. . . .

Still, as this poem concludes, the genuine is in the picture, not the beholder; and

> It comes to this: of whatever sort it is,
> it must be "lit with piercing glances into the life of
>> things";
> it must acknowledge the spiritual forces which have
>> made it.

And so, the test of the genuine is at once in the quality of that which is described and in the description. The reality of the toad is integral with the fact that the garden is imaginary; that someone, as a controlling presence, has imagined it, has furnished it the only kind of setting in which its reality could be wholly known. Commenting on her work, she wrote in 1938, "I feel that the form is the outward equivalent of a determining inner conviction, and that the rhythm is the person." [1]

What then of Miss Moore as the descriptive poet about whom Williams and Eliot wrote? I think that, for all the justness of what each says, each is wrong—simply because he would make literature more than a phase of life. Miss Moore's descriptions, if we study

---

[1] "A Note on Poetry," written as a headnote for a selection from her work in *The Oxford Anthology of American Literature,* ed. N. Pearson and W. R. Benet (New York: 1938), p. 1319.

them closely and give ourselves over to them, will not allow for such an interpretation. *Contra* Williams, she insists on having ideas about the thing; *contra* Eliot, her meditations are tied to and defined by the thing, not released by it. Instances are abounding. Here is a short one:

No Swan So Fine

> "No water so still as the
>   dead fountains of Versailles." No swan,
> with swart blind look askance
> and gondoliering legs, so fine
>   as the chintz china one with fawn-
> brown eyes and toothed gold
> collar on to show whose bird it was.
>
> Lodged in the Louis Fifteenth
>   candelabrum-tree of cockscomb-
> tinted buttons, dahlias,
> sea-urchins, and everlastings,
>   it perches on the branching foam
> of polished sculptured
> flowers—at ease and tall. The king is dead.

Above all, this is exact; and the careful accumulation of curios, mementoes, *objets d'art* is such as at first to appear unending; the end must be surprisingly forceful, as it is; moreover, it is inevitable, the only end. Everywhere there is constant evidence of the poet's controlling presence—in the highly artificial, ad hoc syllabic meter and stanza construction; in the gentle guidance given the reader by such occasional rhymes as swan-fawn; in the seemingly chaotic collections of objects described, as though this were a scene only because the poet can dredge up from her memory such a collection of odds and ends; and in the mere existence of the quotation marks in the first three lines, which signal to us that the poet has appropriated something for her (and our) use. The lines run into each other, forcing a hurried reading, thus forcing a hurried collocation. The movement begins to break with the pause after "flowers." The words "at ease and tall" take us away from the purely artificial nature of what has gone on before; for such words apply as well to living as to sculptured flowers. Then there is a longer pause. And then the meaning is totally precipitated with the last four words, and we recall the "dead" of the second line, now understanding what it has all along implied. Art *can* kill, even—and this is what alarms us—when it would give life.

This is Miss Moore's technique at its most exquisite. Here, as in "The Fish," "Steeple Jack," and "The Plumet Basilisk" among her earlier poems and "Elephants" and "Tom Fool" among her later ones, the meditation is minimal and is made to result, like a sum in addition, from the scene and the occasion. At other times, in poems which I think are not quite poems but, however brilliant, exercises in rhetoric, she allows herself the liberty of meditation as such— for example, in "What are Years?":

> What is our innocence,
>   what is our guilt? All are
>   naked, none is safe. And whence
> is courage: the unanswered question,
>   the resolute doubt,—
> dumbly calling, deafly listening—that
> in misfortune, even death,
>   encourages others
>   and in its defeat, stirs
>
>   the soul to be strong? He
> sees deep and is glad, who
>   accedes to mortality
> and in his imprisonment rises
> upon himself as
> the sea in a chasm, struggling to be
> free and unable to be,
>   in its surrendering
>   finds its continuing.
>
>   So he who strongly feels,
> behaves. The very bird,
>   grown taller as he sings, steels
> his form straight up. Though he is captive,
> his mighty singing
> says, satisfaction is a lowly
> thing, how pure a thing is joy.
>   This is mortality,
>   this is eternity.

The sentiment here is Adamic *par excellence:* with its sense of the great glory in sheer mortality. Yet the poem is made to *argue* its case; and the figurative language functions as a controlling similitude, like an afterthought which reinforces, not develops, its substantial concern. It is significant, I think, that Miss Moore came to publish such a poem and others like it ("In Distrust of Merits" and "Bulwarked against Fate," for example) after she had established her reputation as a descriptive-meditative poet—in the 1940's and after.

Such poems have, besides their intrinsic merit, that of guiding us into an understanding of her *oeuvre*. Truth in these poems *is* an Apollo Belvedere, formal; but the quality of its formality is somewhat eased when they are placed in their proper context.

Such poems point toward her later, and greater, ones: "Nevertheless," "The Mind is an Enchanting Thing," "His Shield," "Amour's Undermining Modesty," "Tom Fool," and "Blessed is the Man." In these poems, Miss Moore's precise sense of place, occasion, motif, and the like is made not to add up to its egocentric meaning but to lead into it. Here she is most like Emily Dickinson, though without Emily Dickinson's range and passion. These poems are so composed as to make for the observation of an aspect of humanity which is prefigured, and no more than that, in something non-human. Observation becomes a means to, not a mode of, insight. Thus:

Nevertheless

you've seen a strawberry
    that's had a struggle; yet
    was, where the fragments met,

a hedgehog or a star-
    fish for the multitude
    of seeds. What better food

than apple-seeds—the fruit
    within the fruit—locked in
    like counter-curved twin

hazel nuts? Frost that kills
    the little rubber-plant-
    leaves of *kok-saghyz*-stalks, can't

harm the roots; they still grow
    in frozen ground. Once where
    there was a prickly-pear-

leaf clinging to barbed wire,
    a root shot down to grow
    in earth two feet below;

as carrots form mandrakes
    or ram's-horn root some-
    times. Victory won't come

to me unless I go
    to it; a grape-tendril
    ties a knot in knots till